All through the Town

Forerunners: Ideas First

Short books of thought-in-process scholarship, where intense analysis, questioning, and speculation take the lead

FROM THE UNIVERSITY OF MINNESOTA PRESS

(Continued on page 77)

All through the Town

The School Bus as
Educational Technology

Antero Garcia

University of Minnesota Press

MINNEAPOLIS
LONDON

ISBN 978-1-5179-1565-0 (pb)
ISBN 978-1-4529-6963-3 (Ebook)
ISBN 978-1-4529-6964-0 (Manifold)

Published by the University of Minnesota Press, 2023
111 Third Avenue South, Suite 290
Minneapolis, MN 55401-2520
www.upress.umn.edu

Available as a Manifold edition at manifold.umn.edu

The University of Minnesota is an equal-opportunity educator and employer.

For the riders of yesterday and tomorrow,
dreaming of new routes to freedom

Contents

Introduction: All through the Town

MONTHS BEFORE THEY BECAME running mates and were subsequently elected president and vice president of the United States in 2020, a testy exchange took place during the first democratic presidential primary debate between Joe Biden and Kamala Harris. Seeking to highlight discrepancies in Biden's legislative record, Harris made a powerful accusation: "You also worked to oppose busing. And, you know, there was a little girl in California who was part of the second class to integrate her public schools, and she was bused to school every day. And that little girl was me." Muddying the line of attack, Biden retorted, "I did not oppose busing in America. What I opposed is busing ordered by the Department of Education."

The exchange made headlines as one of the most effective moments during the debate (even if Biden ultimately prevailed as both democratic nominee and the duly elected forty-sixth president of the United States). As one of the only times that education was even mentioned during the electoral season, Harris's comments humanized the costs of desegregating U.S. public schools and efforts toward providing an equitable learning opportunity for students of all backgrounds. Journalist and creator of the 1619 Project Nikole Hannah-Jones described how the presidential exchange spoke to the central arguments of failed desegregation efforts throughout the twentieth century in a *New York Times* article fittingly titled "It

Was Never about Busing."[1] As Hannah-Jones explains—and as a key argument in this book—busing became a convenient euphemism for desegregation in U.S. schools while also working to expand our school system beyond the one-room schoolhouse. This twinned form of progress has blurred the lines of what buses do and what busing means today.

The school bus is the longest-lasting and most widely felt intervention in public schooling in the past century. It's been wielded as a tool for moving U.S. education beyond rural one-room schoolhouses at the turn of the twentieth century and as a means for directly addressing segregation in the wake of the *Brown v. Board of Education* case in 1954. At the same time, I argue that while its no-frills design belies an archaic mode of transport, the school bus—hissing brakes, clacking windows, blaring intercom, and all—is the most disruptive piece of technology that has shaped the learning experiences of young people. No other comes close. Not the slide projector, the graphing calculator, the computer, or the VR headset.

Most readers may not be accustomed to seeing the utilitarian and archaic bus as a piece of cutting-edge technology. That's because in this book, I approach the bus as technology and examine the histories of schooling and innovation that have left an imprint on the United States. In this way, busing technology refers to the actual school bus as a piece of educational equipment and the cognitive technology of busing to integrate and broaden access to schools. Across the chapters of this book, I detail how the school bus has been operating invisibly as a technological intervention for generations. As a de facto approach to desegregating public schooling and shaping city networks around bureaucratic education systems, the bus is heralded as the most direct pathway toward improving the schooling experiences for millions of children every day. Yet, the bus is not a perfect vehicle for educational reform.

1. Nikole Hannah-Jones, "It Was Never about Busing," *New York Times,* July 12, 2019, https://www.nytimes.com/2019/07/12/opinion/sunday/it-was-never-about-busing.html.

Setting aside the substantial carbon footprint of this intervention for the time being, let's recall what was so effective about Harris's line of attack during that presidential debate; she moved beyond debating if the bus was impactful to instead pointing to the experiences of people like her who rode school buses daily. While educators and policy argue the merits and drawbacks of busing, these squabbles do not typically consider the experiences of the students riding buses, like Harris did, each morning and afternoon. Likewise, policy discussions typically do not define the bus as a particular technological object: why this shape, these features, and these operating structures? The affordances of the school bus as a form of technology and the limitations that come with it have been overlooked in the ongoing use of this mass-produced technology.

The beauty of the school bus as a technology is how, even in its bulky form, it invisibly carries forward effects from one generation to the next. The thousands of hours that people accumulate as passengers to and from school each day—far more commuting time than their non-bus-riding classmates—are a time tax levied on the bodies and minds of predominantly Black and brown young people in America.

As part of my work as a qualitative educational researcher, my research team and I spent an academic year riding a local school bus with elementary and middle school children. On this bus, students spent an average of ninety minutes each way (and sometimes closer to two hours in afternoon traffic) simply to get to school. These students boarded the bus as early as 6:30 a.m. each morning and often did not arrive home until 5:00 p.m. They spent this time sitting, waiting, sleeping, with no access to a bathroom or permission to eat food—a tall order for children and young adults. Bus time contests the perception of school as a fixed set of instructional hours transpiring from 8:00 a.m. to 3:00 p.m. each workday. The bus extended the school day, during which time it educated young people (particularly young people of color) about how to be docile, passive, and grateful for the opportunity to travel *away* from home for education. In this light, consider the power of the school bus as a technological intervention; it transforms who students are and what they assume they are capable of. You cannot presume a laptop or a tablet or educational software to so consistently and pervasively instruct young people in the same way as the bus.

Considering the frustrations that I heard and personally experienced while researching the school bus, I am particularly aware that we could use this piece of technology differently. Every day, as I rode the school bus, I was reminded of better busing solutions whizzing by my window. With minute-to-minute regularity, white charter buses would pass the students, transporting workers to and from the tech giants—Google, Facebook, YouTube, and Apple—that surrounded this area. Spacious, with modular layouts, lightning-fast Wi-Fi, bathrooms, and delicious free snacks, these nonschool buses speak to how transportation has refused to update when it comes to the needs and desires of America's youths. This technology is one of control.

This book looks at the specific features of the bus as a technology, what happens on this vehicle, and the possibilities for transforming this technology for future generations. To take you on this journey—one that shapes the lives of millions of young people every day—we need to first familiarize ourselves with key terms and attributes related to busing technologies.

Busing Technologies

In my conversations with educators, parents, and policy makers, I'm met with an equal mixture of confusion and skepticism around my claim that the school bus is the most powerful form of educational technology modern society has experienced.

For one thing, the school bus is so . . . *old*. It surely can't be the thing we collectively refer to as "technology," can it? When faced with comments like this, I draw on learning scientist and researcher Roy Pea's definition of technology as "any medium that helps transcend the limitations of the mind, such as memory, in activities of thinking, learning, and problem solving."[2] Pea's description reminds us that the humble school bus extends where and how school transpires every day. Adding a slight nuance to Pea's description about the role that educational technology plays in schools today, I want to suggest that there are three broad ways it is utilized in public education:

IT MAKES EDUCATION BETTER. This can include opportunities to broaden learning by illuminating new ways of engaging with material, such as through exploring distant worlds with VR headsets, or by implementing customized tutoring support through a mathematics software program.

IT MAKES LEARNING MORE CONSISTENT. By ensuring all students might receive similar learning experiences using similar tools, educational technology is frequently pointed to as a resource for "leveling the playing field" when it comes to educational opportunity.

IT MAKES EDUCATION EASIER. For students both to access content in multiple modes and to provide teachers with easy-to-deploy curricular resources, the tools of technology make learning easier.

I offer this subjective categorization of the purposes of educational technology pessimistically. Very little of how we have deployed educational technology as a form of intervention in schools has to do with the joy, freedom, or interests of young people or the dignity of a teaching profession beleaguered by years of disrespect. While the entrepreneurs behind technological tools may talk a big game about the agency and engagement their products instill, their bottom line when it comes to digital devices is about profit, productivity, and ensuring global competitiveness. Across more than a century of interventions, educational technology has done little

2. Roy Pea, "Beyond Amplification: Using the Computer to Reorganize Mental Functioning," *Educational Psychologist* 20, no. 4 (1985): 167–82.

to fundamentally change the landscape of schooling. As stalwart educational researcher Larry Cuban wrote, "those who have tried to convince teachers to adopt technological innovations over the last century have discovered the durability of classroom pedagogy."[3] It's no surprise that the classroom of today *still* looks remarkably like the classroom of your childhood.

Entire fields of research, policy, and mainstream media obsessively detail and explore the affordances of new technologies within schools. Admittedly, a large portion of my own academic career has navigated this space. Yet, for all our continued interest in the possibilities of technology, we have not transformed the learning experiences of students in wide-scale, life-changing ways. Sure, we like to spend large swaths of educational budgets on the latest technologies. Tablets, laptops, VR headsets, and wirelessly connected "smart" classrooms all get regular attention as innovations that might revolutionize schools. They will not. Simultaneously, scant attention has been paid to the mundane, dutiful tech that hisses as it stops just *beyond* the threshold of our school entrances.

If we look beyond the classroom, the school bus fits all three purposes of educational technology described previously. Subtly, the bus has been shifting the learning landscape for generations. Despite how noisy, brightly painted, and bulky it may be, the bus is an invisible disruption; its bodily and emotional shifts are accepted by millions of families rather than questioned. It is *because* the bus is not considered a form of educational technology that it has insidiously and persistently shaped the lives of young people nationwide.

In *Border and Rule: Global Migration, Capitalism, and the Rise of Racist Nationalism,* Harsha Walia accounts for the construction and enforcement of state-based boundaries in eras of global migration. She makes clear that the impact of a "border" extends

---

3. Larry Cuban, *Teachers and Machines: The Classroom Use of Technology since 1920* (New York: Teachers College Press, 1986), 109.

far beyond the small space a wall, fence, or invisible boundary circumscribes.[4] Rather, she suggests that a border is a technology that exists and changes the meaning and status of individuals regardless of where they are physically. As a shared social understanding, borders shape the meaning and interactions of people throughout the world. Building on Walia's logic, the influence of the bus as a form of technology persists long after students have completed their morning and afternoon commutes.

Extending Walia's work, I discuss two types of bus technologies throughout this book. First, I detail the physical bus as a form of technology that operates, intervenes on, and supports student learning today. As you may recall from your own childhood, they are brutally functional, no-frills vehicles. The second form of technology is a cognitive one. The role of *busing* in U.S. school systems reorients where, how, and for whom schools operate on a daily basis. Binding policy efforts like school desegregation to yellow school buses turned these vehicles into the primary drivers for diversifying schools and shifting the quality of education. As this book argues, no other form of technology singlehandedly transformed the lives of young people across generations in such a profound and ongoing way. Importantly, these two technologies are interwoven historically and socially. As detailed in the next chapter, the history of the school bus mirrors the history of the formation of U.S. public schooling and, shortly after, the impact of policies around school desegregation.

Riffing on the name of a popular children's book, there is a kind of "magic" in how the school bus consistently moves so many children without substantial halts in operation. There is a trick to moving millions of students millions of miles, extracting millions of hours of time that could be used for learning, sleeping, eating, playing, or dreaming. Like all good magic tricks, buses deceive us

4. Harsha Walia, *Border and Rule: Global Migration, Capitalism, and the Rise of Racist Nationalism* (Chicago: Haymarket Books, 2021).

all by directing the public gaze away from social costs and toward the blinking light of educational equity and opportunity.

A Brief Word about Technology and Buses in a Time of Global Pandemic

It may seem odd to explore the nature of the school bus as a form of educational technology now; it has been operating for decades. Even more recently, a global pandemic has shifted our attention even further away from the seldom considered bus. However, it is precisely because of the invisible nature of the school bus as technology—across time and during social catastrophe—that this book can offer alternate understandings of educational technology and of the school bus. As a means of diving deeply into a particular and often ignored resource, this book demands we imagine a system of schooling that does better. There are other ways of getting children to school, beyond assuming technologies might get our school system out of inequitable pitfalls that have little to do with technology. Rather than seeking alternatives from apps, digital resources, or even from buses, I suggest that innovation and ingenuity must be analog in nature, driven by human imagination and compassion.

I hope that the journey of this book convinces you of the overwhelming power of busing technology on the lives of children in America across history. By understanding the contemporary and historical forces of this innovative device, this book offers us an opportunity to reimagine how technology functions in society today and how we might question who designs the tools we use. In the remainder of this book, I offer a history of how the school bus and the processes of busing in America became so fundamental to public schooling. Tracing its history and physical construction and role in desegregation, the first chapter of this book argues that the school bus is the greatest educational intervention. It has endured a century of operation, rewriting the racial makeup of schools. Next, my research team and I invite you on the daily journey of current elementary school students in chapter 2. We detail a year-long, prepandemic study of student experiences on a public school bus. Building from this, chapter 3 offers a systemic overview of the bus's physical features to argue that the bus embodies the broader societal shifts toward what scholars today call "platforms" in educational technology. Adapting these contemporary metaphors for online tools, I look at how analog technologies like the school bus are constantly reconfiguring school life. Finally, the concluding chapter of this book speaks to the future of bus technology and how schools, machinery, and educational technology might transform the lives of their bus commuters. Settle in, passenger, for a multistop journey.

1. Round and Round: The Journey of the School Bus

With Stephanie Robillard

IN HIS ESSAY "Does the Negro Need Separate Schools?," W. E. B. Du Bois describe what he feels is necessary for Black students to succeed:

> The proper education of any people includes sympathetic touch between teacher and pupil; knowledge on the part of the teacher, not simply of the individual taught, but of his surroundings and background, and the history of his class and group; such contact between pupils, and between teacher and pupil, on the basis of perfect social equality, as will increase this sympathy and knowledge; facilities for education in equipment and housing, and the promotion of such extra-curricular activities as will tend to induct the child into life.[1]

Du Bois outlines what Black families wanted for their children and were not receiving. Segregated school facilities were often dilapidated, teachers were underpaid or undertrained, and the materials were often hand-me-down textbooks from white schools. The fight for desegregated schools was also a fight for equal access to education; it was a fight for Du Bois's vision. Sites like the Mississippi Freedom Schools and the Black Panther Party's Oakland

1. W. E. B. Du Bois, "Does the Negro Need Separate Schools?," *Journal of Negro Education* 4, no. 3 (1935): 328.

Community School—localized, Black-led responses to the prevalence of anti-Blackness in education—demonstrated alignment with Du Bois. These schools provided students with opportunities for a transformative education despite the ongoing inequities shaping American schooling structures.[2]

We start this chapter with Du Bois's vision to illustrate the stakes of what busing has *done* in the United States for nearly a century. Through this idea, we review the history of how the physical school bus came to be, to show how busing technology became inextricably linked with the largest school-based intervention that has ever been wreaked upon young people. In doing so, we offer the history of how the familiar yellow school bus came to be. We illustrate how this physical technology eventually came to function as a cognitive and organizing force for social stratification, desegregation, and ongoing educational interventions throughout the United States.

As a profound example of educational technology, the school bus's role in altering the racial and socioeconomic landscape of schools is perhaps its most indelible and lasting achievement. Intentionally, this chapter explores the history of the school bus and the history of school *busing*—a verb that became grounded in U.S. schooling after *Brown v. Board* in the mid-twentieth century. To fully understand the scope of the school bus as technological intervention across public schooling, this chapter traces the origins of the bus as an object and a sociopolitical force in education.

2. Jon N. Hale, "The Students as a Force for Social Change: The Mississippi Freedom Schools and Student Engagement," *Journal of African American History* 96, no. 3 (2016): 325–47; Daniel Perlstein, "Teaching Freedom: SNCC and the Creation of the Mississippi Freedom Schools," *History of Education Quarterly* 30, no. 3 (1990): 297; Russell Rickford, *We Are an African People: Independent Education, Black Power, and the Radical Imagination* (Oxford: Oxford University Press, 2016); Robert P. Robinson, "Until the Revolution: Analyzing the Politics, Pedagogy, and Curriculum of the Oakland Community School," *Espacio, Tiempo y Educación* 7, no. 1 (2020): 181–203.

Beginnings

Every year, 450,000 public school buses travel more than 4.3 billion miles, carrying 23.5 million children to and from school and school-related activities.[3] These easily recognizable and highly visible bright yellow school buses dot morning and afternoon commutes. In nonpandemic periods, their absence harkens school vacations, and their fall return signals the start of the school year.

The first record of student transport to school in the United States was written in 1886, predating the first automobile by six years. These vehicles were known as kid hacks.[4] Kid hacks were made of wood, sometimes out of repurposed farm wagons. No more than twenty children from local farms would board these vehicles, entering and exiting in the rear to avoid scaring the horses that pulled them. Wood benches lined the sides, keeping the center free. A thin tarp protected students from the elements. Students who did not join this transport either walked to school or were taken there in a family's wagon. These carriages may not seem like much, but they were the beginning of U.S. public school transportation. Twenty years later, kid hacks were motorized as the United States transitioned to automobiles.

Standardization

As the twentieth century unfolded, school buses slowly morphed into the more familiar vehicles that students ride today. Maintaining the basic design of the early models, manufacturers added an additional door in the front and switched to steel framing, while designating the rear door for emergency use only. Buses at this time

3. National Highway Transit Safety Administration, "NHTSA's Unedited Summary of School Bus Report," 2021, https://www.cde.ca.gov/ls/tn/or/nhtsa3702.asp.

4. *Hack* being shorthand for *hackney,* a type of carriage pulled by mules or horses.

ranged in colors, including patriotic hues of red, white, and blue. As there were no national safety standards at the time, school bus features were inconsistent. However, all forty-eight states allocated funds for student transportation. Wayne Works in Indiana, International Harvester in Illinois, and the Blue Bird Corporation in Georgia led school bus manufacturing, which thrived even as the economy faltered at the start of the 1930s.[5]

Enter Frank W. Cyr, a former teacher turned professor with interests in rural education and school transportation. Having received a $5,000 grant from the Rockefeller Foundation, Cyr organized a national conference on school transportation and invited representatives from every state—as well as executives from the manufacturing sector, Dupont, and Pittsburgh Paint—to standardize the school bus.[6] His goal was to compose a set of minimum regulations that would ensure a uniform school bus that was both safe and economical. It probably goes without saying that "representatives" at this convening did not include the actual passengers of the school bus. The history of the creation of the school bus is devoid of input from its clientele. The world of public education has spent more than a century educating, assessing, and transporting young people largely without the input of young adults and children.

The conference created a forty-six-page report that included sections on the school bus chassis and body as well as a section on the school bus driver. The forty-four agreed-upon regulations covered a range of issues, including requiring a speedometer (regulation 18), a fire extinguisher (regulation 6), a first aid kit (regulation 7), and a toolbox (regulation 20) as well as prohibiting a driver's side

5. Harlan Tull, "Transportation and School Busing—the School Bus, History of Pupil Transportation, Issues in Pupil Transportation," https:// education.stateuniversity.com/pages/2512/Transportation-School-Busing .html.
6. "Frank W. Cyr, 'Father of the Yellow School Bus,' Dies at the Age of 95," https://www.tc.columbia.edu/articles/1995/august/frank-w-cyr-father -of-the-yellow-school-bus-dies-at-the/.

door.[7] While these regulations are consistent with modern-day school buses, many of the other regulations have shifted with time as technologies have improved.

The driver-employees on these vehicles were not exempt from regulation either. The portion of the regulations addressing the school bus driver includes recommendations for selecting drivers by ability, such as to "make all ordinary repairs and adjustments and to keep the motor in good working condition."[8] The test for driving includes noting whether the driver is "nervous, overconfident or easily distracted."[9]

The Yellow School Bus

The most publicly recognizable regulation to come out of meetings Cyr organized, though, concerned identification (regulation 9):

For purposes of identification school bus bodies:

1. Including hood, cowl and roof, shall be painted a uniform color, National School Bus Chrome, according to the United States Bureau of Standards specifications with the exception of fenders and trim.
2. Fenders and trim shall be black.
3. Shall bear the words, SCHOOL BUS, in black letters at least four inches high on both the front and rear of the body.[10]

The past one hundred years have seen updates to the interior and exterior of the bus, but the ubiquitous color—"National School Bus Glossy Yellow"—has remained.[11] National School Bus Chrome,

---

7. *Minimum Standards for School Buses,* National Conference on School Bus Standards, 1939.

8. *Minimum Standards for School Buses,* 37.

9. *Minimum Standards for School Buses,* 36.

10. *Minimum Standards for School Buses,* 23.

11. Notably, it is illegal to paint nonschool buses this particular color. It is both one of the most commonly identifiable vehicular colors and the most rare for personal vehicles.

named after the chemical compounds used to create the paint, was originally several hues, as it was difficult to reproduce the exact shades at the time. It was selected for its high visibility, particularly during the morning and evening hours, contrasting with what Cyr referred to as the "camouflage" colors of red, white, and blue. Cyr regarded these suggestions as well meaning but asserted that "they made the buses less visible. And I don't think it really had much effect on patriotism."[12] Chromate was eventually removed from the mixture, as it contained lead, leading to a shift in the paint name while retaining a standardized yellow exterior.

Safety

The two priorities of the 1933 conference were to ensure a safe and economical school bus. Modern advances, including an additional wave of regulations in the 1970s that sought to reduce injury in accidents by including emergency exits and rollover protection, have increased safety. Seat belts remain a safety feature inconsistently implemented nationwide; only eight states require seat belts.[13] Large school buses use what the National Highway Traffic Safety Administration refers to as a "protective envelope" as a means of protecting children. The closely spaced seats with high and cushioned seat backs help absorb crash energy that can occur in larger-capacity school buses.

Additional safety features include amber lights and stop signs affixed to the bus that warn other drivers to slow down or stop. Drivers who ignore the stop sign can be fined up to $1,000.[14] Global

12. Kristen Green, "Prince Edward County's Long Shadow of Segregation," *The Atlantic* (August 1, 2015), https://www.theatlantic.com /national/archive/2015/08/segregation-prince-edward-county/400256/.

13. Rudy Chinchilla, "'Like Eggs in a Carton': Here's Why Most School Buses Don't Have Seat Belts," NBC10 Philadelphia, February 13, 2020, https://www.nbcphiladelphia.com/news/local/like-eggs-in-a-carton-heres -why-most-school-buses-dont-have-seat-belts/2294864/.

14. "School Bus Fines by State," AARP Driver Safety, https://www .aarpdriversafety.org/schoolbusfines.html.

Positioning System (GPS) units have also been a recent addition to school buses, allowing for dispatch centers to monitor the school bus and its location in real time. GPS units allow dispatch centers to notify families or school sites of delays or accidents and can help prevent notable incidents like the 1976 Chowchilla bus kidnapping from ever happening again. While regulations surrounding the school bus as a means of moving children to and from school occurred beginning in 1933, a different dialogue was about to emerge as busing children took on additional meanings.

Leading to *Brown*

As a young girl, Linda Brown would leave her house early in the morning, pass Sumner Elementary, cross busy intersections, and walk through an active railyard to reach the bus stop that would take her to her school.[15] Regardless of the weather, Linda would make the trek, even when tears from the cold froze to her face. After getting on the bus, she and her classmates were driven to their segregated school, Monroe Elementary. Linda Brown was the eldest daughter of Oliver and Leola Brown, the named plaintiffs in *Oliver Brown, et al. v. The Board of Education of Topeka, et al.* in 1954.

Though the Brown family lived in an integrated neighborhood, Topeka schools were integrated only at the secondary level, requiring the bus ride away from her neighborhood to Monroe. Monroe was a fine school, with good teachers and facilities on par with the school white students attended, according to the Browns and other families involved in the lawsuit. Their concern was that only four schools were available for Black students to attend, compared with the eighteen schools for white students.[16] If Black families

15. Linda Brown Smith, "Interview with Linda Brown Smith," video, Washington University, October 26, 1985, http://repository.wustl.edu /concern/videos/1n79h614g.
16. Cheryl Brown Henderson, Deborah Dandridge, John Edgar Tidwell, Darren Canady, and Vincent Omni, *Recovering Untold Stories: An*

became dissatisfied with their schools, or weary of the commute, these eighteen schools would remain inaccessible.

Although the Browns were the titular plaintiffs in the landmark court case, the case itself involved five different lawsuits brought forth by the National Association for the Advancement of Colored People (NAACP). Thirteen families from Delaware, Kansas, South Carolina, Virginia, and Washington, D.C., were the plaintiffs in the case. As a result of the *Homer A. Plessy v. John H. Ferguson* court case,[17] which provided legal ground for racial segregation, school districts were able to establish separate schools for Black and white children. The experiences of these other families paint a vivid picture of what it was like to be educated under Jim Crow. Delaware had only one high school for Black students: Howard. There was no transportation to Howard. Students could ride a city bus with local stops, which took an hour, and then had to walk several blocks to arrive at the school. Brigitte Brown, daughter of one of these bus riders, recalled her mother noting that "they passed a total of three white high schools on the way to Wilmington."[18]

In South Carolina, students also walked to inferior schools, while school buses "were shuttling white children to their white schools."[19] Parents faced retribution for seeking an equal education for their children, including being fired from their jobs. Denia Hightower, whose family was among the 107 parents and children to seek better schooling, remembered that her father, "like so many others, had been fired from his job and was told that he could have his job back if he took his name off the list."[20]

In Virginia, high school student Barbara Johns led a strike to protest the conditions of her education, remarking that white students

---

Enduring Legacy of the Brown v. Board of Education Decision (Lawrence: University of Kansas Libraries, 2018).

17. Plessy v. Ferguson, 163 U.S. 537, 16 S. Ct. 1138, 41 L. Ed. 256 (1896).
18. Brown Henderson et al., *Recovering Untold Stories,* 28.
19. Hannah-Jones, "It Was Never about Busing."
20. Brown Henderson et al., *Recovering Untold Stories,* 66.

"were not cold, they didn't have to leave one building and transfer to another. Their buses weren't overcrowded. Their teachers and bus drivers didn't have to make fires before they could start class."[21] The strike came with consequences. Families were no longer given credit in stores and were threatened with job loss and physical violence. Johns moved in with relatives for her safety; however, the Virginia families remained steadfast. The NAACP appealed each case through circuit courts and then merged the cases into one, which became *Brown*.[22]

Brown Decision(s): Enter Busing

In a unanimous decision, the U.S. Supreme Court sided with the families, overturning the "separate but equal" doctrine affirmed sixty years prior in *Plessy v. Ferguson*. They concluded that, "in the field of public education, the doctrine of 'separate but equal' has no place. Separate educational facilities are inherently unequal."[23] The logistics of how desegregation would occur was decided in the second decision, *Brown v. Board of Education II*. Setting a pace that pleased neither side, the Supreme Court set a guideline of "with all deliberate speed"—allowing for a variety of implementation time-lines and models and, most importantly, approving the use of busing as the primary technology for integrating schools.[24]

This is the general story of schooling in the United States of which most adults are aware: a decision in the 1950s required schools to desegregate, which was a grand move toward equitable learning opportunities for all. This, however, is only the beginning of a very uneven story whose noble outcomes are yet to be achieved. As

21. Brown Henderson et al., 86.
22. Brown v. Board of Education, 347 U.S. 483, 74 S. Ct. 686, 98 L. Ed. 873 (1954).
23. *Brown*, 347 U.S. 483.
24. Brown v. Board of Education, 349 U.S. 294, 75 S. Ct. 753, 99 L. Ed. 1083 (1955).

anyone who's looked closely at schools today knows, educational opportunity in America is very much still cleaved by divisions in race and class. Buses have played a role in both mitigating *and* reinforcing racial and class-based discrimination. For all the bluster around educational equity over more than half a century, schools in this country have remained woefully inconsistent when it comes to determining who gets what educational opportunities.

Prior to the *Brown* decision, students rode segregated buses to segregated schools across segregated areas of the nation. Riding on buses meant they were *bused* to school. With the *Brown* decision, the term *busing* took on this meaning and use, becoming synonymous with desegregation efforts. Advocates for desegregation used the word *busing* to refer to the means by which students were transported to school; however, opponents of desegregation used the term *busing*—as well as *forced busing* and *mandatory busing*—to signify the transport of students as part of a desegregation program.[25]

White opposition to desegregation took on many forms, including boycotting schools and opening private segregated schools. Arkansas governor Orval Faubus famously called in the National Guard to block Black students' entry.[26] Some cities even went so far as to shut down entire school districts to avoid court-ordered desegregation.[27]

Desegregation Busing

To help illustrate the ongoing impact of busing, three communities show how districts responded to the *Brown* decision. The first district, Charlotte-Mecklenburg Schools (CMS) in North Carolina,

---

25. Jeffrey A. Raffel, *Historical Dictionary of School Segregation and Desegregation: The American Experience* (Westport, Conn.: Greenwood Press, 1998).

26. President Eisnehower then ordered them to protect Black students' rights and safety.

27. Green, "Prince Edward County's Long Shadow."

would eventually receive praise for its successful school integration. CMS played a key role in busing becoming a primary way to achieve desegregation. However, initially, like many districts in the south, CMS failed to integrate the schools, necessitating Black families to seek remedy through the court system. The case of *Swann v. Charlotte-Mecklenburg Board of Education* in 1964 eventually reached the U.S. Supreme Court in 1971, driven by the central question of how much jurisdictional power the Court had in overseeing desegregation. In addition to deciding that the Court did indeed have the jurisdictional power, the Court also affirmed the use of busing as a means of desegregation.

White residents of Charlotte were not pleased. Wealthier families responded by enrolling their children in private segregation academies or moving to majority-white towns still unconcerned with busing. Other families participated in coalitions like the innocuous sounding Concerned Parents Association," which adopted practices from the civil rights movement, including staging sit-ins, singing "We Shall Overcome," and electing three anti-busing school board members. They strategically framed opposition to busing as an issue of choice. Newly elected senator Jesse Helms spoke out against busing, labeling it as "discrimination in reverse."[28]

It is important to note that not all Black families were pro-busing. George Leake, a pastor in the African Methodist Episcopal Zion Church, was staunchly anti-busing. Years prior to the *Swann* decision, he was vocal about being concerned only with the education of Black children, seeing no need for integrated schools. Echoing Du Bois, Leake found it more important that Black children had quality facilities and a good education. He hated "the loss of the identity of any predominantly black school."[29] However, as the Court's decision loomed, he was willing to concede that should the

28. Jack Bass, "Oral History Interview with Jesse Helms," Documenting the American South, March 8, 1974, https://docsouth.unc.edu/sohp/A-0124/menu.html.

29. Smith, interview.

Court rule against the district, he would support busing. Later, when opposition to busing decreased, Charlotte-Mecklenburg schools were praised as examples of how integration could work.

Together, Black and white students in the Charlotte-Mecklenburg schools were bused to their new school sites. The bus taking students to West Charlotte High, a historically Black school, transported both Black and white children. Betsy Hagart, a white student who rode the West Charlotte bus, lived in East Charlotte. She was picked up with others from their predominantly white neighborhood and driven west, as the bus continued to add students. By the time the bus reached Black communities, it was often full. According to Hagart, white students gave up their seats because they were intimidated by Black students who entered with a perceived "tough attitude." White students read their body language as being rooted in a sense of insecurity being around white students, "who are, well . . . you know, fairly well dressed and they are not because they came from a project."[30] Hagart's interpretation of her Black classmates' stance fails to consider that the Black students on the bus might resent the now crowded bus or the presence of white students in their formerly all-Black school.

Like Charlotte, the Boston Public School District was a site of a significant court case about busing. In 1965, the state legislature passed the Racial Imbalance Act, which made it illegal for schools to have more than 50 percent minority students. When Boston schools refused to comply, the NAACP again filed suit. District Court judge W. Arthur Garrity determined that when schools in Boston remained segregated, it created a situation that allowed for two distinct and unequal school systems: one for Black students and one for white. With only eleven weeks to prepare, Boston implemented a busing plan that brought white students to predominantly Black schools and Black students to predominantly white schools.

30. Amy Stuart Wells, *Both Sides Now: The Story of School Desegregation's Graduates* (Berkeley: University of California Press, 2009).

Much of the anti-busing organizing in Boston was done by white women motivated by a concern for property rights and parents' rights. Women's groups, such as NAG (National Action Group) and ROAR (Restore Our Alienated Rights), were concerned with property rights, as they feared integration would decrease their home values. As mothers, they felt desegregation limited their ability to care for their children, for example, by rendering them unable to walk them to and from school. Framing opposition to busing in these ways allowed white women to present themselves, not as racists, but as concerned parents. Their organizing was aided and encouraged by southern support. They visited North Carolina to learn from organizers there and invited leaders like George Wallace and members of the Ku Klux Klan to speak to these women's groups.[31] As McRae notes, "'motherhood' was understood to elevate their concerns and grant them a kind of moral supremacy. Maternal politics could be invoked for liberal or conservative causes. But the motherhood claimed by segregationist women—in 1940s Jackson, Mississippi or 1970s Boston, Massachusetts—was tied to their whiteness and class position."[32]

The buses carrying Black children were pelted with bricks, bottles, and rotten eggs on the first day of school. White people yelled at the children on the bus and called them racial slurs. Police dressed in riot gear stood along the roads to school to protect students from the abusive parents. The National Guard was put on alert, and news crews from the major networks covered the story. At the end of the first day, a fourteen-year-old girl named Regina Williams told her mother that she would not go back to the school unless she had a gun to protect her.[33] She did not return to that school. A white teenager

31. Elizabeth Gillespie McRae, *Mothers of Massive Resistance: White Women and the Politics of White Supremacy* (New York: Oxford University Press, 2020).

32. McRae, 237.

33. Bruce Gellerman, "'It Was Like a War Zone': Busing in Boston," WBUR News, September 5, 2014, https://www.wbur.org/news/2014/09/05 /boston-busing-anniversary.

weaponized a flagpole by swinging it toward a Black lawyer entering Boston's city hall. The incident was captured by photographer
Stanley Forman, who won a Pulitzer Prize for his iconic photo.

Unlike the previous two busing plans, Berkeley, California's,
policy did not come about through a court mandate but through
voluntary action. Given that there was one public high school, the
focus of desegregation efforts centered on kindergarten through
ninth grade. The work to move toward desegregation involved support from the NAACP and the Congress of Racial Equity, as well as
community organizers. When the school board voted to desegregate
the junior high schools in 1964, some segments of the population
threatened to recall the board. Although the recall measure failed,
it was enough to cause the district to hold back on integrating the
elementary schools. When the district eventually moved toward
full desegregation, it implemented a busing plan similar to Boston's.
Wealthy white students from the hills were bused to the flatlands,
predominantly occupied by Black and poorer families, and vice
versa.[34] This method was intended to allow for the burden of desegregation to be spread across all students, rather than overtaxing
Black children. However, this was not the case, as proponents of
segregation simply enrolled their children in private schools or
moved their families to majority-white suburban areas.

Busing in Berkeley was different than it was in Charlotte and
Boston because the district was much smaller, so bus rides were
shorter. Doris Alkebulan was a third grader when desegregation
busing began. Her reflections on being a bus rider walk us through
the steps the district took to prepare families for desegregation.
On the first day of busing, she was not as nervous as her classmates
because her parents had enrolled her in a pilot program the year
prior. Dean Fukawa only recalled there being more students on the

34. "50th Anniversary of Berkeley's Pioneering Busing Plan for
School Integration: Berkeley Unified School District," Berkeley Public
Schools, August 26, 2019, https://www.berkeleyschools.net/2018/12/50th
-anniversary-of-berkeleys-pioneering-busing-plan-for-school-integration/.

bus who he didn't know. Anna Clark Foote described it as feeling normal to take a bus to school. Her comment evokes the reflections of Vice President Harris, who also participated in Berkeley's busing program. The vice president described her experience in her memoir, writing, "All I knew was that the big yellow bus was the way I got to school."[35]

Although Berkeley's busing program had a more successful beginning than those in other parts of the United States, it bears remembering why busing was necessary to begin with. Berkeley was a segregated city, with Grove Street (now Martin Luther King Jr. Way) marking the border of the redline districts. When the city banned housing discrimination, three white high school students burned a cross on the lawn of a mayoral candidate. Berkeley High School, the only public high school in the district, was featured in a 1996 documentary that drew attention to academic experiences of students who fell along racial lines: Black students were funneled into one track and white into another. It also documented the tension and violence that often boiled over, reminding viewers that racial strife still existed in the perceived liberal haven of Berkeley.

The "End" of Busing

Looking across the long history of busing, we recognize that the answer to whether busing "works" is far from simple. Several events have undermined efforts to desegregate schools. In the 1970s, a provision was added to the General Education Provisions Act about the use of federal funds for busing. The provision reads, "To overcome a racial imbalance in any school or school system or to carry out a plan of racial desegregation."[36] This provision was only recently repealed by the House of Representatives.

35. Kamala Harris, *The Truths We Hold: An American Journey* (New York: Penguin, 2021).

36. "General Education Provisions Act (GEPA): Overview and Issues," https://www.everycrsreport.com/reports/R41119.html#_Toc256753016.

Under Nixon, the U.S. Supreme Court took a more conservative turn and began to weigh in on (or decline to hear) busing appeals. One example of the Court's influence returns to where busing began—CMS. In 1991, Bill Capacchione, a parent whose daughter was denied entry into a magnet school, sued CMS on the grounds that she was denied because she was white. The case advanced through the system, and U.S. district judge Robert Potter ruled in favor of Capacchione, overturning the *Swann* decision. The Supreme Court decided not to hear the appeal, leaving *Swann* overturned and rendering busing no longer an acceptable means of desegregation. This case undermined the *Brown* decision, as did others, such as *Miliken v. Bradley* in 1974, which banned forced busing across government boundaries, and *Freeman v Pitts*, which loosened oversight over which schools could be deemed sufficiently desegregated.

Assuming there has been an "end" to busing is tied to perspectives of how this verb functions and one's stance toward school integration in the decades since *Brown*. For instance, the nature of U.S. communities could be interpreted as one factor allowing for an understanding of the end of desegregation busing. Massachusetts's Racial Imbalance Law is an example of a legal attempt to redress segregation in clearly segregated schools. In response to the busing mandate, parents moved to predominantly white suburban areas where busing would not affect schooling, or they enrolled their children in private schools. As a result of the decrease in enrollment, school districts with population shifts ceased busing programs. Working around the legislative mandates for desegregation, individuals, cities, and states have found ways to maintain school segregation by *retaining* the efficacy of busing. Like any technology, buses can be as much a means to reinforce educational inequality as they might alleviate it.

Impact

When we talk about "impact" and vehicles, the results can be gruesome, harrowing, and unforgettable. An impact from or with a school bus is exactly what driver's education courses train young drivers to avoid. In this way, let us consider what kind of social impact these vehicles have made across the landscape of American education. Examining the lasting role of desegregation busing reveals both positive and negative outcomes related to the academic achievement and personal growth of millions of students. More importantly, there are less obvious yet still directly related outcomes.

Multiple studies document the benefits all students receive from attending integrated schools, alongside specific benefits for Black youths. Rucker C. Johnson noted that Black students having access to school resources like smaller class sizes uplifts their socioeconomic status.[37] In later research, he found that students who were in desegregated schools attended college at higher rates, earned greater incomes, and experienced less poverty.[38] Vice President Harris pointedly acknowledged the impact of busing on her life trajectory in a tweet on July 9, 2018: "Two decades after Brown v. Board, I was only the second class to integrate at Berkeley public schools. Without that decision, I likely would not have become a lawyer and eventually be elected a Senator from California."[39] This sentiment led to her personal critique in the presidential debate that opened this book. Additional benefits bused students have noted include feeling comfortable in predominantly white workspaces, specifically not feeling intimidated.[40] Such nonacademic opportunities for learning might be seen as benefits of desegregation as an educational intervention. We can interpret these findings as speaking to how school buses—as forms of technology—orient students of

37. Rucker C. Johnson. *Long-Run Impacts of School Desegregation and School Quality on Adult Attainments,* publication w16664 (Cambridge, Mass.: National Bureau of Economic Research, 2011).

38. Rucker C. Johnson and Alexander Nazaryan, *Children of the Dream: Why School Integration Works* (New York: Basic Books, 2019).

39. Kamala Harris (@KamalaHarris), "Almost two decades after this landmark ruling," Twitter, May 17, 2017, 2:08 p.m., https://twitter.com/KamalaHarris/status/864950669861687296.

40. Wells, *Both Sides Now.*

color into white cultural practices. However, they do so with little consideration of what might be lost, sacrificed, or suppressed by naturalizing white spaces. In this way, we can interpret the "wins" of desegregation as an embrace of whiteness rather than as achieving the multicultural values typically celebrated by politicians and the media. Although students who were bused to school benefited in the long term from improved facilities and extracurricular activities, they suffered in the short term from being in schools that were hostile toward them. Many of the first waves of Black students who desegregated schools regretted having been part of that class and later attended historically Black colleges.[41]

Perhaps the greatest loss coming out of desegregation is related to Black staff and faculty. Prior to *Brown,* segregated schools were staffed mostly by Black teachers and administrators. With the *Brown* decision, many Black students were able to access schools that had improved facilities and better materials than those that they had previously attended. However, when administrators at these predominantly white schools hired additional teachers for the increased enrollment, they did not look to Black teachers. Black teachers had predominantly supported the *Brown* decision because they wanted their students to gain access to better resources. However, as Siddle Walker describes, these teachers "traded aspiration and advocacy for access to the resources white schools had."[42] Even in

---

41. Karida L. Brown, "The 'Hidden Injuries' of School Desegregation: Cultural Trauma and Transforming African American Identities," *American Journal of Cultural Sociology* 4, no. 2 (2016): 196–220; DeBerry, "For Some, School Integration Was More Tragedy than Fairy Tale," *NOLA,* May 30, 2019, https://www.nola.com/opinions/article_82d5155e-78f4-5234-b03a -d5566c880c9d.html; Sam Turken, "Little Soldiers: Members of Norfolk 17 Discuss Their Experiences during School Integration," WHRO, February 25, 2020, https://whro.org/news/local-news/7199-we-were-the-soldiers -two-members-of-norfolk-17-discuss-their-experiences-during-integration.

42. Cindy Long, "A Hidden History of Integration and the Shortage of Teachers of Color," NEA, November 3, 2020, https://www.nea.org /advocating-for-change/new-from-nea/hidden-history-integration-and -shortage-teachers-color.

cases in which districts used both facilities, white families would opt for private schools or move before sending their students to historically Black schools. Their decisions decreased enrollment and, again, resulted in a loss of jobs for Black teachers. Even though the *Green v. County School Board* case in 1968 outlined markers (thereafter known as the Green factors) that indicated whether a school district was desegregated, the focus was primarily on student enrollment. Black teachers can also offer social-emotional support for Black students, particularly students who are not attending predominantly Black schools. But Black teachers have never recovered from the loss of employment stemming from the *Brown* decision.

Driving Away from Technologically Deterministic Solutions

The kid hacks at the beginning of this chapter—proto-buses cobbled together in rural areas—were sparked by technological innovation. As buses turned into motorized carriages of an eponymous yellow hue, these vehicles became the fundamental form of school transportation that persists today. Likewise, in becoming the mechanism for legal jurisprudence, the school bus became the innovative form for addressing (often ineffectively) racial inclusion in this country. As a form of social technology focused on addressing school integration (e.g., "busing") and as a modernized vehicle indicative of twentieth-century progress (e.g., the bus as an object), the histories of busing technology developed in parallel. As a result, the school bus's twinned forms of technological progress were fused in its ongoing role in schools today.

Determining the effectiveness of busing to bring about desegregated schooling requires asking what busing's end goal was. If it was only to transport students, that absolutely happened. Buses successfully brought students to and from school, even when the National Guard was required to protect the route. But if this technological intervention was intended to be a vehicle to provide equitable education—to meet students' academic needs while affirming their inherent value as people—then it failed. Once students arrived at school, though they may have learned required academic content, they were not protected from physical and emotional abuse by their peers and teachers. Though busing did provide all students, Black and white, with opportunities to engage in cross-cultural friendships and expand their racial awareness,[43] is that enough to counter the "frequent discrimination, hostility and rejection" they also endured?[44]

More than sixty-five years after *Brown,* vestiges of redlining remain, school demographics mimic pre-*Brown* racial demographics, and students continue to ride buses to get to school. All three branches of the federal government have undercut the fiscal and legislative support for integration. Alternative plans that replaced busing—magnet schools, charter schools, and student placement plans—have not achieved the Green factor for measuring full desegregation.

There are other possibilities for addressing structural inequalities linked to segregated schooling. Richard Rothstein suggests that it is inconceivable to think that education reform can happen without addressing neighborhood segregation.[45] Mathew Delmont suggests that large cities can revise school district lines. He notes that redrawing district lines is controversial even in liberal places like New York—let alone conservative places—because "primarily white parents and upper-middle-class parents, purposely buy homes in

43. Roslyn Arlin Mickelson, Stephen Samuel Smith, and Hawn Amy Nelson, *Yesterday, Today, and Tomorrow: School Desegregation and Resegregation in Charlotte* (Cambridge, Mass.: Harvard Education Press, 2015).

44. Valerie Strauss, "What Black Students Who Were Bused Said about Their Experiences," *Washington Post,* July 8, 2019, https://www.washingtonpost.com/education/2019/07/08/what-black-students-who-were-bused-said-about-their-experiences/.

45. Richard Rothstein, "For Public Schools, Segregation Then, Segregation Since," Economic Policy Institute, August 27, 2013, https://www.epi.org/publication/unfinished-march-public-school-segregation/.

areas where they know they're going to be sending their children to schools that are largely segregated."[46] These measures require dismantling historic systems of inequality at a local level, and the technology of school busing has proven ill equipped to combat the resilience of wealth and whiteness in this country. Reverting the interventions of busing technology is not easily done; unlike stripping a computer for parts or uninstalling a series of apps, the journeys paved by the school bus cannot be rerouted quickly or seamlessly.

Jesse Jackson summed up the congressional opposition to desegregation in a 1982 opinion piece. His opposition to busing wasn't about legal overreach or fiscal responsibility. In Jackson's opinion, it wasn't the bus that was Congress's problem. The problem they had was with Black people. Du Bois's essay on whether Black children would benefit more from separate schools sets up a binary that Black families still face in the fight for equity of schooling. He wrote that a "mixed school with poor and unsympathetic teachers, with hostile public opinion, and no teaching of truth concerning black folk, is bad. A segregated school with ignorant placeholders, inadequate equipment, poor salaries, and wretched housing, is equally bad."[47] There are ways of providing Black students with education that supports their academic needs and affirms their cultural background. Busing Black youths and other youths of color across cities in an attempt to diversify and desegregate schools has not been the solution to the problems that civil rights activists have sought to redress. Instead, the role of educational technology has simply muddled the shape, context, and operations of schools for generations. The millions of hours that students cumulatively spend sitting on buses each day can be thought of as an educational tax extracted from students of color in a country still anxious about

46. "A History of School Busing," *Weekend Edition Sunday,* NPR, June 30, 2019, https://www.npr.org/2019/06/30/737393607/a-history-of-school -busing.

47. Du Bois, "Does the Negro Need Separate Schools?"

accountability and student presence. As we explore in the following chapter, their hours on buses are not, however, devoid of meaning. Students learn complex lessons about schooling and socialization in the hours riding to and from school every day.

2. Move on Back: The Experience on a School Bus

With Jorge Garcia and Stephanie Robillard

IN POPULAR CULTURE, the yellow school bus is often associated with fun, learning, and adventure. Ms. Frizzle and her Magic School Bus—mentioned in this book's introduction—entertain countless children. The appropriation of the yellow school bus in Oakland's "hyphy" movement has ensured that it retains a whimsical place in our collective memory. Media depictions of budding romance offer nostalgia-tinged glasses through which to interpret adolescent and childhood days spent blissfully on a bus with friends. Even when the school bus is boring, it is a place for daydreaming. As a form of technology, the bus is enchanting.

Our research draws a different, more nuanced understanding of the reality of commuting for countless children. First, let's acknowledge the obvious: commuting three or more hours a day is exhausting for anyone. As adults, we can often determine when and how we will complete a journey and decide what we will eat and where breaks will occur. By comparison, children commuting to school on a yellow school bus have little agency over how the journey will unfold. The rules governing the bus mean that children are unable to take care of their most basic needs, including thirst, hunger, and bathroom breaks. On a journey ostensibly benefiting students, it is striking that their daily comfort and well-being are generally disregarded.

Fundamentally, our research encourages educators, parents, and general members of a schooling community to recognize a truism about technology: when we center the *tools* of educational technology over its users, we must question who these tools benefit and at what scale. Particularly as the intended users of school buses, students weren't asked for their input when it came to the design and implementation of school buses, as described in the previous chapter. These vehicles are taken for granted as part of the cost of attending public school today.

As a way of framing what it feels like for these children to ride a yellow school bus, we traveled with one group of children as they responded to a playful invitation to imagine how they might better design their commuting experience. That is, we asked a number of them what they might change about their bus-riding experience if they were in charge. We found their answers telling. It is striking that, essentially, what the children voiced were basic human needs.

One elementary school–aged child spoke of the sleepiness they felt. Getting to the bus stop in time for their 8:00 a.m. class meant getting up and leaving their house at 5:00 a.m.—early, indeed, for a growing child. Another child wished the bus would stop at a drive-through restaurant and buy food for everyone. School bus rules didn't permit students to eat or drink during the commute, essentially meaning that most students either skipped breakfast or nibbled snacks as they hustled to class. The same child pointed out the cameras installed inside the bus and described the ways they were invasive.

Children shared what we call the *need for creative engagement*. We pause here to explain that we were invited onto this school bus to help administrators imagine ways to better support the academic learning needs of school bus commuters. While students sought creative outlets, their administrators were also searching for additional learning time from kids stuck in a metal tube each morning and afternoon. Administrators saw this time as a period during which they might alleviate boredom. One idea a school official offered was to give each student a camera to take and share photos (though some students had mobile devices, phones weren't as ubiquitous as they were among their older peers).

Students were asking very basic needs to be addressed during their time on the school bus. During our months of research, which we detail in the rest of this chapter, we regularly marveled at their capacities to cope. We had not yet become attuned to the idea that this bus—as it was configured and designed by policies and historical legacies that address the injustice of contemporary segregated school systems—was inhumane. When given even a limited opportunity to speak directly to the open-ended question of how they might change things if they were in charge, students asked for basic human rights: sleep, food, privacy, and creative engagement. The absence of these elements troubles a rosy vision of this educational technology.

Throughout this chapter, we detail a year of learning and listening with kids on a bus. We highlight how assumptions of adult expertise often got in the way of the dreams and desires of the kids. In sharing examples from our research, this chapter questions what technological interventions actually do. As a larger critique of tools like busing, we take the historical grounding of the previous chapter as an opportunity for understanding the chaotic lived experience of kids on buses today. We also offer an interactive vision of how research, practice, and policy are constantly shaping and shifting the experiences of students in school settings.[1]

---

1. There are few other qualitative studies of children's experiences on the school bus. We do, however, acknowledge the influence of Ira W. Lit's work on the framing of our study. See Lit, *The Bus Kids: Children's Experience with Voluntary Desegregation* (New Haven, Conn.: Yale University Press, 2009).

Meet the Kids

The students we rode the bus with were like many of the count-less students in the United States who ride a bus in the wake of desegregation efforts. In our particular case, we rode alongside approximately sixty kindergarten to eighth-grade students from the Bellwood community.[2] They were of different ethnic and language backgrounds (65 percent Latinx, 25 percent Pacific Islander, and 10 percent Black, based on available school-reported information) and spent 90 to 120 minutes on the bus in the mornings to get to school and another 90 to 120 minutes in the afternoon to get back home. These were the children from Bellwood whose families had opted in to a voluntary program to transport children to nearby districts. It was launched in the mid-1980s, after years of litigation by parents of the region. Led by a parent of a Bellwood student, several dis-tricts near Bellwood were sued for unconstitutional segregation in the schools. As a result, better-performing districts were obligated to reserve space for children from underresourced areas of the region. For more than thirty-five years, the region's districts have maintained this program. In turn, during this time, children from Bellwood continuously spend up to twenty hours a week on a bus to access the promise of a better education.

As the transportation program was an effort to desegregate, it is important here to note the role of busing not only in desegregation efforts but also in policies of segregation, as discussed in the pre-vious chapter. In *Building Inequality: The Spatial Organization of Schooling in Nashville, Tennessee after Brown,* Ansley T. Erickson[3] asks, "how much of the burden of desegregation should children be expected to shoulder?" Children most negatively impacted by segre-

2. In accordance with our research protocols, all student, school, and geographic names are pseudonyms in this chapter.

3. Ansley T. Erickson. "Building Inequality: The Spatial Organization of Schooling in Nashville, Tennessee after *Brown," Journal of Urban History* 38, no. 2 (2012): 247–70.

gation have had to shoulder the burden of desegregation efforts and policies. Busing reveals itself to be a function of both segregation and desegregation regimens.

Riding Along

Our study was born from districts' desire to better understand the academic learning needs of students routinely commuting from Bellwood to the Hays and Jackson School Districts. Recognizing the time spent on the school bus, a superintendent reached out to Antero wondering how his previous research on mobile media[4] might show how to better support bused students. Our research team was invited to support the district as it tried to find ways to enhance the bus-riding experience. We wanted to understand what the children participating in this program experienced every day. With a broad mandate to explore and pilot interventions, we took up different kinds of playful learning experiences with students after first spending time sitting and *feeling* life on the school bus. We planned narrative-based games and project-based learning opportunities and choice-based reading. As we describe subsequently, some of our efforts proved promising in the limited confines of the bus. But we were continually thwarted by the sheer noise and discombobulation of the bus experience.

We had been warned by some district administrators that the bus was an *unruly* space, as behavioral issues were regularly reported. In contrast to the misbehaving youth about whom we were warned, however, we discovered a rich ecosystem of interactions, learning, and coping that children had crafted for themselves. It took us a while to adjust, as mixed in with the delight of engaging the children with activities and conversations, some of us experienced motion sickness, headaches from the cacophony of unrelenting engine and road noise, and utter brain fatigue from exhaustion. Riding the

4. Antero Garcia, *Good Reception: Teens, Teachers, and Mobile Media in a Los Angeles High School* (Cambridge, Mass.: MIT Press, 2017).

school bus is an intense experience that we too often discount in our vestiges of memory. If we, as adults, felt the exhaustion of this occasional research experience, just think of the physical and emotional toll this commute takes on America's youths. As a research team, we spoke often of how the children managed this day in and day out, as a passage to school and back home.

Our planned activities for exploring learning and engagement with young people were often thwarted by the sheer noise of the bus. In response, we brought instruments to measure sound levels and worked with students to measure how loud the bus was at any given time. We engaged these kids as they wrestled with making sense of the data. We also listened closely to the ways children used, modified, or superseded sound as they crafted their own aural space in the cacophony of the bus ride. This proved to be a fruitful approach, as we began to see sound used as a means to create community and engage in acts of resistance. We began to recognize the malleability of sound and the power of sound to mediate spaces.

Veratl

As a research team, we were interested in constructing unique experiences for young bus riders that might rival the time their non-bus-riding peers were enjoying at home or in after-school programs. Was it possible for the bus ride to be a joyful and fun experience? After riding alongside these students for a quarter, we designed Project Scout, a project-based learning experience about an extraterrestrial being who was interested in communicating with fellow travelers. Veratl—an adolescent, gender-neutral, amorphous being from outer space—would initiate contact with students, inquire about their lives, and gain an understanding of what these bus-riding travelers' lives were like.

We created a backstory for Veratl; they would need four crystals to power their spaceship to return home. These crystals represented data we would collect along four themes: curio (curiosity), communo (community), chrono (chronology), and carto (place).

We recruited a fellow researcher to play the role of a space scientist tracking extraterrestrial communication. To inspire curiosity, we placed QR codes around the bus, hoping that students would use their digital devices to access a message from Veratl (which a team member recorded using a voice modulator). Immediately, these ludic efforts floundered. Younger students were frightened by the message, whereas others immediately assumed it was fake and lost interest. Not deterred by flagging interest, we planned to press forward with a year-long engagement within this alternate reality game. Of course, it was not meant to be; when it comes to learning on a school bus, there is never a smooth or easy journey.

The end of Project Scout began within weeks of its beginning. One reason we phased it out was our inability to maintain engagement with the project when we were not present. Even then, we noticed that a smaller portion of the older students participated only because we asked them. They were, in fact, doing us a favor. We were troubled that students were participating out of a sense of obligation. This was their space, and we were coddling them in ways we did not intend. Then, another, more significant reason for ending the project emerged: one of our research team members, Miroslav, had developed a burgeoning friendship with one of the older boys, named Josué. Miroslav would often sit near him and talk about his day, gaming, or other interests. Josué was not interested in Project Scout and believed the entire project to be fake. After our fellow researcher dodged the direct question about this project repeatedly, Josué stopped talking to any of us. This project we imagined to be so engaging ended because we realized that we were forcing it on students. We were unintentionally impinging on their time, alienating them, and perhaps violating an unspoken agreement about our relationships. To be clear, Project Scout wasn't all that different from the ways we burden students in schools *every day*. We impose school expectations and technological interventions on the lives of students constantly, with little opportunity for their input, as we presume expertise. Adults seemingly know what's best, a premise that our time on the bus suggests is dubious.

Sound Measurement

Findings from Project Scout prompted us to iterate and imagine different ways of learning with the bus passengers. Said differently, we wanted to put our finger on what shaped so much of passengers' experience on the bus: sound. How could we attune to this presence and quantify its imposition? What would emerge for students if they approached noise as scientists? Our study explored student sensemaking based on the creation and interpretation of sound on their school bus. We worked alongside students to capture and interpret sound levels on the bus. We began to see how students used sounds to create community, exercise agency, and make meaning of their surroundings. Moreover, students used sound to counteract the pervasive drone of the bus itself.

Our explorations of sound measurement and data afforded students an opportunity to reflect on and reinterpret their lives and activities on the bus. Utilizing multiple handheld sound meters, children on the bus took decibel readings and observational notes about the moment of the readings. We worked alongside them to measure sound levels on the bus and engage in meaningful explorations with their collected data. Nearly one hundred data points were collected over four weeks of student-led sound collection on the bus. In the context of the broader understanding of the bus as educational technology, this activity helped elucidate the designed affordances and conditions of the school bus; what it enables and constrains in the lives of its users are often invisible.

We compiled the student-collected data and provided each student with a handout that summarized key elements of their data. This generated dialogue and multimodal meanings, including emotional responses to the sound pressure levels on the bus in relation to other sounds, speculations on why certain areas inside the bus were louder or quieter than others, questions about the geography of sound along the bus's route, and critiques of how the data were represented in our summaries.

Through sound data measurements, students allowed us to coconstruct a soundscape. Students then reflected on, contested against, and negotiated meaning around the soundscape. The summary of the data they captured became a sounding board for students to understand the subjective ways that data—on a bus, on a standardized test, or on a national census—are collected and utilized. In this way, the data acted as a prompt for students to vocalize their own perceptions of the sonic texture inside the bus. As an example, we offer Jamal's insight; Jamal was one of the few Black bus riders, and he expressed frustration by our data summary's suggestion that his school's bus stop was the loudest. As student resistance was often in conflict with adult perceptions of permissible sound, Jamal's voiced concerns spoke to perceptions of being "loud" and its implied negative stereotype of Black people in America.

We found the children deepening their analysis as they spent more time looking at the summaries of the data and discussing them. Above the drone of the bus, a group of riders discussed the data, and several students expressed concern that the sound pressure levels on the bus might be unsafe, based on a chart we provided to students showing them a range of daily sound levels encountered. Students pointed to the subjectivity of data collection and how different data points meant different things for different people. These discussions of the measured data raised an opportunity for the youths to reflect on sound and to see it in stark relief, as they were previously not attuned to it in this manner.

One middle school student, Alejandra, offered a critique of the data collection method; she doubted the authenticity of the highest recorded sound pressure readings and was dubious of how her fellow bus riders were choosing to measure sound. She shared that she had observed measurements being taken while the user was shouting loudly and directly into the sound pressure meter and suggested that data captured and interpreted on our collaborative spreadsheet should reflect this deviation. Alejandra was also curious about limitations and differences between the types of sound pressure meters. She proposed that we create a protocol to ensure uniformity in methods of collecting readings. Absent those methods, she felt that any reported findings were probably not accurate.

Inspired by the feedback from students like Jamal and Alejandra, several of the elementary school students decided to seek the extremes of both high and low sound pressure inside the bus. With eyes on their sound pressure meters, they held their breath in anticipation to see how low their measurements could go. We saw other students also engaged as listeners and as intentional nonmakers of sound. The students then pushed the envelope further and proceeded to collectively scream. The shrieks sounded joyful and cathartic; their sonic smiles could be heard throughout this activity. Youths embraced the opportunity to turn the inside of the bus into an after-school playground. The sound pressure was physically palpable, and some of our research team covered their ears, while the students seemed unbothered. This moment of unrestrained release blended student-driven inquiry with the overriding of sonic norms on the bus. At least for the moments of this activity, the sound became a source of collective joy. Later in the journey, the activity shifted from collective screaming to individual contests in which the winner was crowned the "scream queen."

Friendship, Mentorship, and Traveling Companionship

Alongside understanding how students can make meaning of the sonic phenomenon of the bus, we explored how youth relationships were supported in the aisles of the bus. Demonstrated camaraderie expanded the affective spectrum experienced by the students on board the bus. As the bus picked up students from schools and dropped them off in different neighborhoods, some friendships were born inside its noisy yellow shell. In our time on the bus, we saw the kind of light affection one might expect from years of sharing a morning and afternoon ritual. Children would often read in pairs, curled into the bench seats and tucked below the high seat-backs, carving out an incrementally quieter space together. Some would lean in toward each other to talk, share a device's screen, or design, fold, and fly paper airplanes. Other students would sit high and rotate in their seats to engage another area inside the bus. We also saw the evolution of more critical and engaged relationships:

> Gabriyel held a worn notebook in his hand, reciting lyrics from a page that was pocked with crossed out phrases, erased, and written over. He strained his voice over the bus's counterpoint and the playful taunts of his peers. As we listened and watched, another student used his Chromebook to play instrumental tracks, with an app that made the keypad a virtual drum machine. Gabriyel was experiencing a comprehensive evaluation and coaching session. Gabriyel shared with us that he had been working on this passage for several days, and we noted his resilience. Most of the unfolding peer feedback was laced with jeers and laughter. "That doesn't even rhyme!" "You sound tired, why you so tired?" "Do it on beat, why you not on beat?" Gabriyel would listen to the advice, quickly scribe new phrases into his notebook, then exclaim, "Okay, okay, I'm ready!" This continued for the better part of an hour, and his delivery, composition, rhyme structure, and content became more refined.

The students created a safer, engaging space of shared vulnerability within their aural bubble, something we've explored in further academic analysis.[5] They did it over the din of the typical student chatter and the ever-present eighty to eighty-five decibels of noise inside the bus. Their care and guidance helped Gabriyel refine a piece of writing while honing his reading of the piece and its vocal performance. His tenacity appeared to impress the older students; when they tried to model for him what he should sound like, they experienced for themselves the difficulty of rapping for longer than one verse. This small group of young composers, coaches, and choreographers pushed the boundaries of how communities were sustained as they constructed a peer-led collaborative learning space inside the bus. This same small group of students

5. Antero Garcia, Stephanie M. Robillard, Miroslav Suzara, and Jorge E. Garcia, "Bus Riding Leitmotifs: Making Multimodal Meaning with Elementary Youth on a Public School Bus," *English Teaching: Practice and Critique* 20, no. 3 (2021): 398–412.

laughed together at Gabriyel's progress, groaned when he fell short, and waited excitedly for his revisions. These shared experiences bolstered their relationships by tending to their relational connections above the noise. Though it is not typically cultivated, busing technology *can* foster community and forms of empathetic civic engagement. It is a malleable technology for social good, if we choose to utilize it as such.

Entertainment on the Bus

Staying entertained was of utmost importance to students on the bus, as it is for many commuters. These students found ways to entertain themselves and have fun. Although a segment of bus riders always immediately put on headphones, listened to music, or watched videos, most students chose to play games. The youngest would play hand games that required coordination, knowledge of the rules, and quick thinking to meet the math or rhyming expectations. In the back of the bus, a group of seven or eight students would play virtual card games against each other over mobile applications. These students' conversations would often be interrupted with cheers or groans, depending on who had played what type of card.

An additional source of entertainment for the children was music. While some students were able to plug in to their own devices, many relied on the radio preferences of the bus driver. Radio stations would prove a contentious issue, as older students would ask for a song to be turned down just after younger students (seated closer to the driver) had requested for the volume to be turned up. The younger students would also sing songs loudly. While their singing would begin matter-of-factly, as soon as they realized it irritated their older bus-riding companions, they would sing louder, even if it was "Frosty the Snowman" on a March afternoon.

Sound did not always divide the students though. As part of Project Scout, we brought personal headsets that connected to a device transmitting sound, like a private intercom system. Although we initially played snippets of Veratl speaking to the students, we eventually switched to music. Children would call out songs that they wanted to hear, and we would play them by connecting our phones to the transmitter. We eventually made a playlist of songs for them. The headsets reduced the noise so noticeably that the bus driver commented that we should bring them every time. The only exception was Lil Nas X's "Old Town Road," a huge pop hit at the time. Recognizing the opening chords, students immediately jumped in singing in unison, startling the bus driver and our research team. The spontaneous joy and delight in that moment were never again replicated to the same degree, even as the bus riders listened to other popular songs.

The Student Costs of Busing

The study described in this chapter was halted in March 2020 as the world as students and adults knew it came to a halt. The global pandemic offered a reprieve from the lengthy commute these students took each day. In doing so, it also cut off the youths of Bellwood from social interactions with their school peers and their city. Extra hours of sleep and recreation were gained as socialization and access to school resources were lost.

To be clear, adult surveillance was a constant problem for students throughout the study. Though we've chosen to center student experiences throughout this chapter, the role of adult power was a constant pressure for young people, just like in schools. The design of the bus, as explored in the next chapter, centers the safety and command of a driver. They can surveil and project their voice to all riders. They simultaneously control what transpires inside and outside the vehicle.

Although this chapter has examined how children applied ingenuity to manage protracted, ill designed conditions, we still are left to wonder, who shoulders the burden of addressing broken systems? Are these technologies conferring basic human needs? Are these technologies conferring dignity on the participants as a rule (rather than as an exception)?

3. Beep, Beep, Beep: The Design of the School Bus

THE BUS HISSES IMPATIENTLY as its doors accordion open. In front of you lie three steps to cross the threshold from land to vehicle. You pass the driver as you make your way up corrugated metal and rubber—all scuffed blacks and metals and yellows. The pallet of bus colors is simple, drab, utilitarian. Schools and teachers will spend small fortunes on murals, posters, and decorations to make their campuses inviting and welcoming for students. The design of the bus, in contrast, aspires only to *function*. Little is inviting about the environment other than the felt urgency to get on so that you might sooner arrive at your destination. A twice-daily experience of sound, color, smell, and sensation, the bus is a felt object that students interact with daily, from the bolted seats to the rattling windows.

In chapter 1, we reviewed the history of the bus, its construction, and its sociopolitical relevance. After that, my research team and I described how time on school buses is actually spent by the young people riding one of them today. In this way, my coauthors and I explored the contexts around and within the school bus. Building on the research in these two previous chapters, here I make an up-close examination of the physical, designed features of the bus and interpret their meanings. As should be clear by now, the design of the bus has been relatively static for nearly a century. Your own memories of time spent on the bus look remarkably similar to students' present-day experiences. The palimpsest-like marks that the patterned vinyl seats left on your bare legs are felt similarly for students riding buses today. Likewise, the clacking windows that require two hands to raise or lower still vex youthful fingers today and will continue to do so for years to come. It may not feel appealing in our empirical reality or in your memories, but approaching the school bus as a designed object reveals the expectations we place on students today. Technologies we introduce into public schooling, such as the bus, mirror what we value in the future generation of young people we educate.

Reading the School Bus

How do we come to know the meaning of the objects around us? How do they reflect their intended and *actual* uses for individuals who interact with them? This chapter is an invitation to look closely at the tools you interact with by scrutinizing their histories and contested visions. Even the mundane must be placed under this lens. As Galen Cranz writes in a book-length work about the humble chair, "most people don't think about chairs much one way or the other, because they are part of our surroundings, meant to support us silently and constantly, without attracting much attention."[1] Though it may be loud, take up substantial space on the street, and play a fundamental role in your family's daily schooling processes, the school bus has adroitly operated "without attracting much attention" as well. If this vehicle has generally escaped public, scholarly, and policy scrutiny, so, too, have the individual components within the bus.

Like your favorite book or magazine, I suggest that we "read" the bus as a text—scrutinizing its composition, function, and hidden and explicit intentions. My reading of the school bus is done with

---

1. Galen Cranz, *The Chair: Rethinking Culture, Body, and Design* (New York: W. W. Norton, 1998), 93.

an eye toward the possibilities of educational technology writ large. It is intended as a kind of open-ended activity that could be done with educational stakeholders. From superintendents to teachers to students to parents, reading the design of a school bus offers an opportunity to revisit what is taken for granted in daily school life and question how we've come to accept and operate buses for a century. In this way, I am adapting Shor's approach to having college students interpret the chairs in their classroom and their intended uses.[2] In his guided dialogue, students connect design to intent: "The chair is a hard, unyielding object, so it's difficult to relax in. Why are you prevented from relaxing in class? Because you'll fall asleep, students answer." Shor adapts this approach from a tradition of critical literacy rooted in dialogue around a particular artifact or motif. By replicating this exercise with you, reader, I invite you to meander with me through the at once familiar and now imagined bus you remember from your childhood.

Take your seat. The vinyl benches lack the seat belts you've come to expect in nearly every other U.S. vehicle. As discussed earlier, this exclusion is intentional, and safety for student lives is embedded in the design of these awkward benches of seating. As you try to stretch in the seat you've taken, you notice only paltry inches of separation from the seat in front of it. The seats on school buses are a snug fit for an adult body. These seats are intentionally made for *smaller* bodies. Depending on age, schools might cluster two or three children per bench. As an adult, you find your knees jutting into the vinyl in front of you, and you skew your legs diagonally, taking up leg room in the central walkway of the bus (despite the driver's warnings to keep this area clear). Even if you were smaller, the sharp angles of seat and back, the unforgiving *stick* of the seat material, and the obstructed views would still be uncomfortable. These vehicles prioritize utility over comfort and sociality. They

2. Ira Shor, *Critical Teaching and Everyday Life*, 1st ed. (Boston: South End Press, 1980).

quickly load a large mass of students and *move* them to their intended destination; the experience of the journey itself is a secondary consideration at best.

Looking around, there doesn't seem to be much else to the bus. No arm rests, no storage space underneath or above the seats, and little else to see or fiddle with other than the rattling windows next to you. The lack of amenities, too, is chalked up to safety concerns— though this doesn't stop other forms of public transportation from offering more versatility.

Perhaps the bus feels sweltering; earlier start dates often mean that bus rides fall in the muggy month of August. Opening the windows on this standard bus is a choreography of digits: simultaneously pressing in tabs on both ends of the window, assuming they are willing to play nice today, guiding fingers, then working to raise and lower the window. These windows are not supposed to be adjusted once the bus is in motion, and so the decision of how much to open or shut a window depends on physical capability, permissibility, and a capacity for predicting the changing climate of a morning or afternoon commute. Could these windows be redesigned? Of course—look at literally any other vehicle's window design and you can see the agency we *could* afford students when it comes to their window options. The limitations of access to fresh air are a part of the technological decisions made for students by adults that are not required to regularly ride these vehicles anymore.

Like almost all other aspects of the bus, the floors, ceilings, and walls are little more than corrugated steel and bolts holding together sheets of metal. Other than mandatory signage at the front of the bus and warnings not to meddle with safety equipment—a hatch in the roof that can offer egress, in an emergency, for example—there are no texts or pictures to capture your eye in this bus.

To be clear, these features are the result of *choices* made for this particular object. And these were choices made by adults presuming they know the needs of children. While the wisdom of age guides how we construct schooling expectations and safety, such decisions are made without regard for young people, their ideas, or their desires. For all of the emphasis on literacy development and academic and social growth in schools, the blank walls and unimaginative design inside the bus are grounded in arguments of safety. However, these arguments are made in contrast to calls for well-being and happiness for young people. Could students customize and design space on a bus? Could they see texts or screens or sounds that affirm their lived experiences? Of course. But such possibilities are absent within the drab text of the bus as we have collectively come to know it. Such calls might be inferred as wildly impossible based on our assumptions of what buses are *supposed* to look like. So let's step outside the bus for a moment.

Let's look at the blinking red lights that signal that the bus has stopped at our destination. We notice that a stop sign has flipped from the side of the bus, warning other drivers to halt until the lights stop blinking.

While we might take buses for granted, they maintain incredible social power. They shape how we interact on roads, and as drivers, we adjust our behavior. Both the robotic appendage swinging from the side of the bus *and* the agentic choice of a driver cause this change in behavior. In his 1960 treatise *Crowds and Power,* Elias Canetti describes a symphony conductor as an example of the most powerful kind of individual. This person, standing in front of a small army of musicians, with their back to an even larger crowd of eager audience members, controls—demands—silence and attention from everyone in the room: "there is no more obvious expression of power than the performance of a conductor."[3] In their use of blinking lights and stop signs, bus drivers, too, wield this power. They surveil and control behavior within the bus and halt traffic and trouble existing flows of cars outside of the bus as well. Busing technology is designed to be helmed by an individual and to alter the behavior of *everyone* in and around it.

3. Elias Canetti, *Crowds and Power* (New York: Farrar, Straus, and Giroux, 1960), 394.

In a seat elevated and distinct from the benches in the rest of the metal tube, the bus driver is surrounded by a complex array of gears, buttons, wheels, knobs, mirrors, vents, lights, and speakers. Theirs is, understandably, a weighty job. Though school bus driver isn't seen as a high-status job in today's society (and neither is the job of schoolteacher, mind you), it is a stressful, high-stakes job. Schedules of expectant parents and educators buckle against the ebb and flow of traffic. On most buses, the driver is also the only adult present. Like a teacher who takes on the responsibility and caregiving for young people in loco parentis, the driver cares for all while their eyes and attention remain focused on the road ahead. Like a conductor aware of an attentive audience but focused on the guiding strokes for a set of musicians, the driver maneuvers a willing vehicle toward school while coaxing students into safe and docile behavior.

As an all-encompassing experience, the bus is a platform for directing the experiences of a substantial number of students during their schooling lives. Likewise, the bus is an infrastructural part of how schools fit within society. Buses open a pathway for discussing and understanding contemporary perspectives on social uses of technology. As a physical representation of how platforms operate, the school bus fuses seemingly old technology with contemporary anxieties about competitiveness and educational equity.

Platforms in Education

The past decade has seen the rise of "platform studies," including what some scholars have referred to as the "platformization of education."[4] Within today's online systems, platforms are considered "digital infrastructures that enable two or more groups to interact."[5]

---

4. Carlo Perrotta and Ben Williamson, "The Social Life of Learning Analytics: Cluster Analysis and the 'Performance' of Algorithmic Education," *Learning, Media, and Technology* 43, no. 1 (2018): 3–16.

5. Nick Srnicek, *Platform Capitalism* (Cambridge: Polity Press, 2017), 43.

Considering how embedded online networks like Facebook and Amazon and Google might be in the full spectrum of social life, Van Dijck et al. describe contemporary shifts to engaging with these tools as a move into a "platform society."[6]

For educational research, platform studies shifts debates away from praising the advantages of individual online tools. It instead reveals how a site like Khan Academy or Classroom Dojo, as broader learning environments, situate and redesign teacher practices and student interactions. As a familiar site that many might know for its online tutoring and enrichment, Khan Academy does not merely support what happens in classrooms. Rather, platforms are *environments,* and, just like in the rest of the world where our time is spent abundantly on platforms like Amazon and YouTube, school life is being transformed by the ways they operate.

Understanding how platforms have reshaped schooling today is necessary and, I believe, overlooked when considering the role of educational technology. As my colleague Phil Nichols and I have explained, "when teachers think of such platforms as tools, rather than digital spaces, they tend to lose sight of important questions about the kinds of educational environments they want to provide and the kinds of interactions they want to create among students."[7] We argue that educators must pay attention to how our interactions and attention have been pulled to platforms and away from the vast wilderness of tools and online sites. Nichols and I describe three ways to interpret the role that platforms play in classrooms:

THEIR SOCIAL USE: how a resource is intended to be used and how is it *actually* used

6. Jose van Dijck, Thomas Poell, and Martijn de Waal, *The Platform Society: Public Values in a Connective World* (Oxford: Oxford University Press, 2018).

7. Antero Garcia and T. Phil Nichols, "Digital Platforms Aren't Mere Tools: They're Complex Environments," *Phi Delta Kappan* 102, no. 6 (2021): 14–19.

THEIR DESIGNED FEATURES: the underlying design decisions for a given platform and what kinds of activities these decisions embolden or hinder

THEIR MATERIAL RESOURCES: the energy, materials, and labor that allow a platform to successfully operate

These three lenses reveal how a software product like Google Docs—popular in classrooms for word processing—might be intended to allow teachers to assign, review, and grade student writing. However, as an *actual* use, many students use the chat feature embedded in the product to socialize with peers while still appearing to be on task in a classroom. Likewise, examining a resource like Twitter, it becomes clear that features such as liking, replying, and retweeting a message limit what "counts" as civic communication on a popular platform that has yielded long-term sociopolitical consequences. Furthermore, the role of content moderators—the thousands of unseen and underpaid laborers who review violent, racist, sexist, and pornographic images to shield the public's view of this material—allows us to recognize that platforms are powered by people and their physical and emotional labor.

The idea of platforms taking up substantial space across educational landscapes is by no means new. As Nichols and I have further argued, "even though it is common to talk about, or evaluate, platforms in terms of what they do (e.g., delivering goods and services), understanding them requires that we also grapple with how they do it—that is, the ways they mediate relations among users, service providers, and other technical systems."[8] This is a *relational* view of platforms that situates them within a broader picture of schooling and technology today.

Talk of platforms and the current, messy state of educational technology is well and good. However, where the rubber meets the road, both literally and figuratively, is in recognizing that platforms

---

8. Phil Nichols and Antero Garcia, "Platform Studies in Education," *Harvard Education Review* 92, no. 2 (2022): 209–30.

aren't new, nor are they solely digital and online. The rumbling, stop sign–blinking, window-chattering, vinyl-seat-leg-dimpling bus can be understood *as* a platform that disrupts and newly "mediates relations among" children and systems of schooling.

School Bus as Platform

Although platform studies in education may be intended to speak to present tools, resources, and mediating impacts of technology today, it also shines new light on past tools. For example, as my colleague Roberto Santiago de Roock and I have argued,[9] the contemporary description of platformization offers a retroactive viewing of technological interactions in nondigital spaces. Furthermore, the contexts of "platforms" illuminate broader orienting practices that persisted in corners of society long before Myspace, Facebook, and YouTube brought the term into digital parlance. For instance, classrooms and schools can be interpreted as platforms. Like an online social network, a classroom has given rules and expectations that orient what people do within the space and what is permissible. This reading offers new lines of critique for the systems and processes by which students are schooled today.

Taking the three lenses from earlier, we can interpret the classroom as a platform intended to orient youth bodies into specific spaces for intended outcomes (though student ingenuity perpetually reorganizes school spaces). Classrooms are designed for specific kinds of bodies and present texts through a curriculum that affirms particular racial and sociopolitical identities. We can see classrooms that draw on the resources of teacher labor, unseen custodial vigilance, and curricular material—from books to tablets to furniture—produced at large scale with few opportunities for customization. Once we can recognize the classroom as platform,

---

9. Antero Garcia and Roberto Santiago de Roock, "Civic Dimensions of Critical Digital Literacies: Towards an Abolitionist Lens," *Pedagogies: An International Journal* 16, no. 2 (2021): 187–201.

we can in turn consider the school bus as the ultimate platform that makes schools today function. But first, let's take a quick detour and consider the metaphor at hand.

As a label, "platform" has been picked up by Silicon Valley in a way that erases its original definition. At least for the next few paragraphs, set aside the social media tools and online learning management systems and e-commerce behemoths that have come to represent platforms. Instead, recall the temporary, raised space you stood upon as you embarked from one setting to another. This platform—a diving board, a terrace for viewing a skyline from the top of a building, a subway station stretch of concrete—was a space that was intended for temporary and transient use. You might linger in these spaces, but you don't *reside* in them the same way your online activities might be confined to a very small handful of online platforms.

The ubiquitous iconography from the London transit system reminds us, when boarding or exiting a train, to "mind the gap." We might stumble, lose our footing, or leave belongings behind in the transition from one space to another in the world of analog platforms. The bus, in this way, is a platform of several layers. Like online systems for grading and attendance, the school bus is fundamental for the operation of daily, schooled life. At the same time, the bus *is* a physical platform that temporarily holds young people as they are moved from one location to another. Both in literal parlance and in the theoretical trappings described previously, the bus is a powerful platform continually shaping students' lives. Furthermore, as fundamental components on which the operations of schools and policies like (attempted) desegregation are built, networks of school buses winding their ways across the dimpled landscape of America each day illuminate these objects as infrastructure on which our systems of education rely.

Broadening the scope of platforms allows us to imagine technology as more than the accumulation of stuff connected to the internet. In general, a reading of the classroom or the bus as technology illuminates our need to more intentionally recognize the full range of educational technology at play. Like a black light that exposes stains and detritus invisible to the naked eye, a platform schema reveals how intentional designs and considerations have perpetually reshaped schooling in ways that reinforce power, limit student agency, and restrict learning opportunities for young people.

Though there is an immediate need to think critically about how data collected from the lives of ever-surveilled young people are used, this doesn't mean we can look past the ordinary and less flashy ways we suppress student learning opportunity and socialization. Returning to the data shared in chapter 1, the fact that busing might reorient racial and sociopolitical interactions across the lives of bus riders is important. As I wrote this chapter, I was continually struck by the history of the first chapter of this book. Particularly, I was reminded that bused Black youths reported not feeling intimidated in predominantly white work environments.[10] More than any other technology, the cultural influences of the bus on student perceptions, beliefs, and workplace behavior are staggering. These influences are the result of designed decisions that tax the social and emotional lives of Black communities. What might be seen as a benefit is also an internal negotiation for each young person about who they might be and who schooling expects them to become as they step off one platform and onto another. Considering this ongoing transformation, an emphasis on understanding educational platforms is not simply about understanding what new (or old) technologies do but also about understanding contemporary anxieties about these technologies.

What's Left Behind?

In his 2021 monograph on the role of the filing cabinet as a pervasive form of information technology, Craig Robertson argues that the inauspicious office equipment transforms, consolidates, and dictates

10. Wells, *Both Sides Now.*

the practices of business interactions and memory.[11] Like a bus that shifted where and how students went to school, the filing cabinet has reshaped offices and their activities. It is worth recognizing that the filing cabinet's introduction first in the United States in the 1890s, then later as a staple of commercial offices globally, closely tracks the metaphorical and literal rollout of school buses across the United States. These technologies speak to broader societal shifts in an era of industrialization. Although the filing cabinet is perhaps slowly being replaced by digital storage racks, the memory moving into digital contexts, the bus has remained the stalwart analog interloper in the lives of youths today.

Educational Technology in Analog

By looking back at platforms and "old" tools, the school bus reimagines the meaning of educational technology. It invites us to revisit what it is, where it is used, and the kinds of lasting effects it might make in society and in the lives of young people. If the school bus is indeed a profound reinterpretation of educational technology, we must recognize that it is largely not a *digital* tool that has been reshaping student experiences for many generations. Rather, as it is a humming engine controlled by a human driver who dictates the use of the bus and its activities, I want to center the *analog* role of tools, people, and imagination that guide what happens in educational contexts today.

Intentionally moving away from learning in schools that emphasizes digital practices, I call for an embrace of analog tools and interactions. Too often, the past thirty years have focused on the oversold promise of blinking screens, internet-enabled devices, apps, and software that are typically not created with the input and insights of students and teachers. However, the digital stuff

11. Craig Robertson, *The Filing Cabinet: A Vertical History of Information* (Minneapolis: University of Minnesota Press, 2021).

that occupies classrooms and fills hours of student instruction has not substantially improved the lives of the kids in schools today. This claim may be contentious, but if we look at the considerable differences that impact educational opportunity in this country by race, gender, and socioeconomic status, technology has not fulfilled its academic promise. Furthermore, if we are to look at the social ills that plague the United States beyond schools—broken partisan-shaped government, increasingly hostile climates of anti-Blackness, and the unrelenting threat of climate catastrophe—digital tools in schools have failed even at prompting meaningful conversation (let alone action) about the great existential threats facing our students.

To be clear, no digital tool will "fix" any of these issues. Rather, as the busing platform demonstrates, human interactions and empathy might advance our educational system closer to justice and action. These are *analog* practices. Such analog relationships—fostered on buses, in classrooms, and in broader civic society—speak to where and for what ends educational technology must play a supportive role. The rapid shifts that occurred in 2020 because of the global pandemic have drastically demonstrated how educational technology can be understood, reframed, and redesigned. As disastrous as the pandemic has been, the possibilities for new kinds of technological uses and innovation are more apparent than ever. How we move forward and take up the future of the bus as a form of educational technology hangs precariously on our willingness to learn about flexibility and human-driven contexts of learning in the wake of the pandemic. Though these might be seen as policy issues that are framing the future, the time waiting and persisting on school buses is a reminder that relationships are at the center of what good learning looks like, and these are, often, placed on cruise control while an infatuation with educational technology inhabits the driver's seat.

4. Open and Shut: The Future(s) of the School Bus

SCHOOL BUSES have substantially shaped the lives of children, the design of school spaces, and the wide-scale operation of public education in America. Yet many questions remain. Have the operation of these vehicles and their designs improved the lives and traveling experiences of the youths who get on them each day? In the context of a legacy of busing that emerged post-*Brown,* has this approach to desegregation actually done justice to historically marginalized children in America? As the first three chapters of this book have explored, there are no easy answers to these questions. The resounding shrug about the impact of busing on American schooling is damning when it comes to understanding how we value the time and dignity of students.

Take a tool, apply it, move on—so goes educational technology in this country. The bus is not without exception. It has promised to "fix" segregated schooling by powering up fleets of buses and let them (slowly) dilapidate. Unlike computers or slide projectors or software that gets updated with newer versions, the bus has quietly persisted because no substantial updates have been offered. It is not in the logistical, academic, or financial interests of innovators or policy makers to find alternatives to the shuttling of youths in this country. Built on a legacy of displacement and dispossession, this form of mobilizing youths toward specific geographies for schooling is a distinctly American experience. Referring to this busing process as one focused on *American* schooling, it is important to acknowledge that this label comes with the understanding that buses and the schools toward which they maneuver are part of and contribute to the settler colonial enterprise of U.S. public schooling writ large. These buses are a colonial technology, reinforcing where school takes place with disregard to land and nonwhite sovereignty. As we consider alternatives, updates, and new approaches to busing in the United States, it is necessary to build on the understanding that buses drive on land that has been taken from Indigenous communities, transporting young people to schools that reside on the same. The tapestry of inequitable socioeconomic distribution that necessitated busing more than half a century ago was woven from the same loom that founded this nation on land theft and chattel slavery. These are not contexts that live *just* in the past—the presence of settler colonialism hulks in the corners of every encounter in schooling today—nor are they divorced from the kinds of changes we might imagine collectively. From land rematriation to the curricular opportunities to broaden learning about and alongside Indigenous pedagogies, the too often overlooked voices of present Indigenous communities must shape how we design, transform, or even abolish busing technologies.

Furthermore, perhaps *because* people have feelings of nostalgia tied to school buses and how they signal an American schooling experience, there has been little effort to substantially transform how these buses operate. In contrast to the bright and shiny new technology brought into classrooms every few years—smartboards, laptops, tablets, and VR headsets—changing the transportation and sorting technology of schooling just doesn't carry the same pizzazz as what Silicon Valley's purveyors of cool may be peddling. Whereas questions about how to improve *school* buses are often met with disinterest at the policy level, insights about public transportation and busing offer ideas about how we could collaboratively transform busing technology and systems—if we collectively wanted to.

Throughout this book, I've tried to explain the contexts of these two interwoven forms of busing technology. As the mechanical wonder of the idling bus shoulders the means of confronting desegregation, the bus expands how technology is understood in educational contexts—learning happens through, because of, and about buses constantly, even if most people look past them as little more than an accepted utility. And this is where transformation could occur: we've taken for granted that this is how schools are *supposed* to operate, and so we refuse to update our perspectives from one generation to another. Sure, we could update the bus itself—make the vehicular technology a little smoother (and we'll look at some examples of this in action later). However, such changes fundamentally assume that buses and busing are necessary for how schools must operate. What would it mean to design our school systems as busing agnostic? Or to utilize the bus *as* the school?

For several years, my wife was the outreach manager for a rural library. Among her responsibilities were driving, operating, and managing the library bookmobile. Watching the gigantic vehicle serve communities—through story times for children, programs for adults, and other civic goods—I was constantly reminded that our assumptions of what mobile technologies matter in and for schools are extremely limited. What would it mean to actually harness busing technology as a central factor in schooling opportunity? Leaning more fully in this direction or more fully away from the use of buses—either way would at least shift our conversations and decision-making about buses. The status quo right now? It's not good enough. We assume the inflexible nature of buses now, as we did in the past and as we will in the future—unless we seek to leverage the disruption in front of us.

In *Better Buses, Better Cities: How to Plan, Run, and Win the Fight for Effective Transit,* Steven Higashide describes the seven basic criteria that satisfy people when it comes to public transportation (like city bus systems).[1] Based on multiple surveys, these criteria

1. Steven Higashide, *Better Buses, Better Cities: How to Plan, Run, and Win the Fight for Effective Transit* (Washington, D.C.: Island Press, 2019).

are worth considering in light of the operations of school buses throughout the United States. Perhaps with exceptions for their reliability (principle 4) or for some routes that pick up students directly in front of a family's residence (principle 5), it is striking that none of the criteria that Higashide describes is consistently met by the school busing systems in America:

1. **THEY GO TO INTENDED AND DESIRED LOCATIONS.** Yes, school buses take students to the schools to which they are required or choose to go. However, schools in America leave much to be desired and improved upon. Considering how real estate listings include information on local schools, a desirable school would make the necessity of arriving at it by bus obsolete. The students in Bellwood described in chapter 2, for example, willfully get on a bus hours before school starts not because they desire to go to a school many miles away. Rather, they take buses because they are the most viable option for providing educational opportunity in the eyes of their parents.

2. **THEY OPERATE FREQUENTLY.** With a single pickup and drop-off time in most situations, buses for school children do not offer any timing flexibility. The frequencies of bus rides and routes are largely out of the hands of young people and their families. Bus schedules are dictated by school schedules, which are also inflexible and generally unresponsive to the needs and interests of young people.

3. **THEY OPERATE REASONABLY FAST.** Traveling safely along the same roads and highways as regular commuter traffic, school buses are about as quick a commute as is possible. While it's arguable that they are much faster than walking or biking to a distant school location, their necessity within current educational systems blinds us to recognizing that public transportation to a closer school system—ideally within one's immediate neighborhood—will always be faster. In this way, I want readers to question what counts as "reasonable" when we ask young people to interface with busing technology today. How much time and how quickly students get to a location are useful considerations. However, the speed of commuting is always tied to a social construction of geography that separates youths from meaningful learning opportunities in their surrounding neighborhoods.

4. **THEY OPERATE RELIABLY.** In contrast to every other principle on Higashide's list, school buses might be close to a paragon of reliability. For more than a century, they have operated in generally the same form, just traveling consistent routes. Like the U.S. Postal Service might struggle with budget and labor demands, school buses and their drivers have weathered ongoing financial challenges to operate reliably. In this way, unlike a dated laptop or tablet that may not be capable of running contemporary software, it is hard to imagine a school bus becoming obsolete in today's learning environment. This is both a feature of school buses as technology and a recognition of how stalwart the societal imagination might be about the fixedness of dated technology for school "operating systems."

On the other hand, although the bus runs reliably on a daily, weekly, and annual schedule, my experience working with young people on the bus described in chapter 2 illuminated the regularity with which students would arrive to school or home late because of commuting delays. From unexpected traffic to the bus driver pulling over to discipline students, the school bus frequently arrived later than scheduled times—an irritation that the students had come to expect.

5. **THE SERVICE GETS YOU WITHIN WALKING DISTANCE OF YOUR INTENDED DESTINATION.** Aside from potential pickup locations at student homes, school bus routes—particularly for young children—often require additional commuting for parents to get students to pickup locations. Yes, schools get the convenience of buses dropping off their students directly at their locations, but this is only half the service. The pickup and drop-off within a home community—such as for the students described in chapter 2—often require parents to travel additional distances, sometimes waiting in parking lots for long stretches of time when the operation of school buses was not as reliable as expected.

6. **THEY OPERATE COMFORTABLY AND SAFELY.** Particularly referring to the experiences noted in chapter 2, students may be physically safe in the vehicles in which they are housed. Yet, given the opportunity to sleep, eat, and freely use a restroom *instead* of riding a bus, these are far from comfortable operations.

7. **THEY OPERATE AFFORDABLY.** When it comes to understanding the *cost* of busing, the financial costs must be considered alongside the costs of student time and meaning making. I recognize

that buses have not seen substantial updates because their costs are covered by schools (and in turn by tax bases). Yet, we still must consider what is extracted from student lives during their time on buses. Too, we should tabulate the ecological footprint these buses have made over their near century of operation. What might seem relatively cheap in terms of impact must be weighed against the long-term costs that allow such busing systems to operate. Like the heuristics of platform studies in the previous chapter, we must question the material resources and human capital that have enabled busing to persist.

My research team and I experienced a surreal feeling while riding the school bus with the students described in chapter 2. Our mundane ride through traffic to and from schools meant looking at the passing scenery, during which time we saw *other* buses: pristine white charter buses took the same major thoroughfares that guided our bus to its destination each morning and afternoon. If you have been in the Bay Area or Silicon Valley recently, these upscale buses are probably a familiar presence to you. It is clear that there are *better* alternatives to the traditional yellow school buses—students just aren't valued enough for us to invest in these options.

Higashide's list is helpful for municipal considerations of public transportation, and his book offers a clear vision for centering busing when considering better ways for cities to operate. At the same time, his list reminds us that comfort and the value of time are reserved solely for adults in this country. As tools that function for our nation's most vulnerable individuals, school buses simply do not heed the voices and desires of their users—something that has not changed for decades.

On Dignity

Taken together, the U.S. implementation of school busing fundamentally disregards the dignity, comfort, and agency of young people. This is not unique to how our society responds to the academic and learning needs of young people; time and again, we strip youths of their say in the broader operations of their civic landscape. Strikingly, it is through the seemingly benign school bus that they lose their dignity. This book illustrates how educational tools—like school buses, computers, or digital platforms—shape and redefine student life.

Though we can pessimistically interpret the impacts of educational technology, these tools do not exist within a bubble. They are always taken up within the sociopolitical contexts in which students are immersed. Across U.S. history, it is the young who have led change. The civil rights movement was largely youth driven. In recent years Black Lives Matter, the March for Our Lives movement, and the Global Climate Strike have spoken to the importance of youths' dreaming and agency, even as digital and analog educational tools surveil and impede them. Young people's dreams for social and civic progress have not been diminished by the draconian approaches of educational technology. Fundamentally, the physical technology of school buses remains unaltered. By looking at how the social technology of sorting and moving young people across this country has led to little actual improvement, we must ask, just how much do U.S. policy makers *actually* care about young people today?

Buses and the "New Normal"

If a central argument of this book is that the school bus has been the most disruptive form of educational technology in U.S. schools, it is telling that it took a global pandemic to temporarily halt its ongoing impact on the lives of millions of children across the country. In fact, I would argue that it is because busing stopped that the instructional tools of learning—online video conferencing software and learning management systems—finally got the attention that skeptics and enthusiasts were calling for. Anxieties around "learning loss" and the quality of online education were hashed out in real time. Messily, they continue to find uncertain purchase in the virtual classrooms of global pandemic as I write this book.

A few years ago, it would have been impossible to imagine schooling in the United States without a busing system. It took a rapid and chaotic response to global pandemic to slow the daily busing commute. However, once busing halted for the better part of the 2020–21 school year, it turns out it wasn't so easy to restart. The current, not-quite-post-pandemic status of busing continues to be stalled. Just as myriad staffing shortages from the pandemic greatly burdened classrooms, a substantial gap in bus drivers is still prohibiting young people across the country from actually getting to school.

In the days when I was finishing the first draft of this book, in early October 2021, a friend in Portland casually mentioned how school buses had upended her family's daily experience. Because of the shortages noted here, every day, either my friend or her husband rearranged their morning and afternoon schedules to drive their kids the lengthy route to their school. As she described this, she noted that the more heartbreaking part of this journey was seeing other students waiting outside "for a bus that was never going to come." Students *wanting* to go to school were left in the literal dust of those whose families had the labor and time flexibility to drive students along routes that weren't in operation (i.e., failing principle 4 on Higashide's list). A local news station reported, "In an email to parents on Friday, Portland Public Schools announced that they canceled 13 bus routes to Benson and Lincoln High schools and 16 routes with different pickup or drop-off times for the foreseeable future."[2]

What is transpiring in Portland is also occurring across the United States. The *Philadelphia Inquirer* reported, "Philadelphia School District officials warned the community about worsening school bus driver shortages this summer and shifted start times over

2. KPTV, "Portland Public Schools Cancel Bus Routes, Parents Left Scrambling," KPTV, September, 21, 2021, https://keyt.com/cnn-regional /2021/09/21/portland-public-schools-cancel-bus-routes-parents-left -scrambling/.

community and school objections to streamline operations. The district is even offering families $1,500 annually to drive their children to school instead of putting them on a yellow bus."[3] Likewise, NPR reported about the impact of furloughs during the pandemic creating shortages throughout the country.[4]

Meanwhile, educational technologists, seeing an opportunity, have started to intrude on the domain of the yellow school bus. While the systems of busing are saddled with labor shortages, technology companies are creeping closer to automating aspects of schooling previously the purview of busing technologies. As reported at the start of the 2021 school year, Bay Area districts are handing over the proverbial keys of their busing system to private companies: "The San Francisco Unified School District has awarded Zūm, a startup that wants to upgrade student transportation, a five-year $150 million contract to modernize its transport service throughout the district."[5] The promise of Zūm is to move to an electric fleet of vehicles (in future years) and modernize the tracking dashboard of buses. Platforms and the allure of shiny new buses at a future date promise to offload the responsibilities of busing to someone else. America's bused youths are going to be someone else's problem to deal with and, likely, for a little bit less money. It is hard not to be cynical of the motives of transportation companies given the immediate shift back to the inequitable conditions of schooling in these precarious times. Even under the banner of working in a "new normal," the same old conditions of schooling remain remarkably trenchant.

3. Chinchilla, "Like Eggs in a Carton."

4. Anya Kamenetz, "National Survey Finds Severe and Desperate School Bus Driver Shortage," NPR, September 1, 2021, https://www.npr.org /sections/back-to-school-live-updates/2021/09/01/1032953269/national -survey-finds-severe-and-desperate-school-bus-driver-shortage.

5. Rebecca Bellan, "Zūm Wins $150M from San Francisco Schools to Modernize and Electrify Student Transport," TechCrunch, July 29, 2021, https://social.techcrunch.com/2021/07/29/zum-wins-150m-from-san -francisco-schools-to-modernize-and-electrify-student-transport/.

The Hollow Promises of Educational Technology

We were promised flying cars and a world without crime. Instead, we got more surveillance and further restrictions on our bodies and cognitive freedoms. The dreams of technological progress far outweigh what actually transpires in classrooms, schools, and society writ large. The platforms that mediate so many of the interactions of students speak to what we've given up of ourselves and how we've abdicated our responsibilities to young people. They deserve more than the wireless tools and algorithmic learning opportunities that have ceded actual pedagogical innovation.

We can now recognize the school bus as a cognitive technology that reorients our assumptions of where schooling occurs and how. The bus demonstrates the juxtaposition between America's promise of educational progress its actual enactment. Describing the school bus and its impacts on civil rights in America, Dee Schofield writes, "It is ironic that the familiar yellow school bus, for many a source of pleasant childhood memories, has assumed the properties of the serpent in Eden, spreading havoc and destruction wherever it goes."[6] As we watch nicer buses operate and fancier new tools brought into classrooms (at the cost of investing in teacher expertise and student interests), the intended uses of technology in schools come into focus: digital tools are about power.

The bus has been powering systems of education for generations, dictating who gets educated and where. It continues to power student experiences, orienting young people to the surveillance of their bodies and the limits of what they might do. It powers educational policies and funding decisions. Even more broadly, the school bus is powering city landscapes and parent relationships with schools. They demand energy consumption considerations and are powering the geographic and spatial considerations of municipalities. Think

6. In Jo Ann Mazarella, *Making Your Busing Plan Work: A Guide to Desgregation* (Burlingame, Calif.: Association of California Administrators, 1977), 2.

of the huge lots that house buses and the ways school parking lots have been designed to ensure that they can easily maneuver them. The school bus powers cities and systems of schooling.

We were promised computer-assisted learning experiences that would locate student bodies virtually in metaverses limited only to one's imagination. We remain benched on school buses taking us on journeys that restrict multiple dimensions of human agency. We let this happen because we've grown complacent about the status quo and nostalgic for how things *used to be*. Those happy feelings you might hold for the school bus in your heart? Those are also nostalgia for eras that originated legacies of harm and racism. Popular media has a long history of romanticizing forms of technology and casting them in the light of adolescent coming-of-age importance: Walkmans, boom boxes, record players, and jukeboxes are tools that typically convey technology-mediated, fuzzy memories of the past. The bus is like that too. It may not look like much, but it is a "charisma machine" in the same way that Morgan Ames describes a mid-2000s infatuation with the one laptop per child movement.[7] If we are going to transform and *improve* the lives of students who currently ride on buses, we need to disregard charismatic technology and a nostalgia that assumes this is how things should be. Students today deserve so much more.

Beyond the "Antiquated Shackles" of Yesterday's Buses

In unveiling his Interstate Highway System in 1954, which would reconfigure transportation across America, President Dwight D. Eisenhower declared a vision of an America empowered by mobility and forward progress: "We are pushing ahead with a great road program . . . that will take this Nation out of its antiquated shackles of secondary roads all over this country and give us the types of

7. Morgan G. Ames, *The Charisma Machine: The Life, Death, and Legacy of One Laptop per Child* (Cambridge, Mass.: MIT Press, 2019).

highways that we need.... It will be a nation of great prosperity, but will be more than that: it will be a nation that is going ahead every day." I've continually thought about Eisenhower's words because his highway system enabled the busing technologies that have been covered throughout this book. The promise of a "great road program" has led to countless hours of student lives dwindling as passengers awaiting moments of learning, friendship, and civic engagement.

In listening to administrators discipline kids as part of the research described in chapter 2, it wasn't uncommon for students to be warned that riding the school bus was a privilege that was afforded to them—a privilege that could be, and, in response to certain behavioral incidents, was, taken away from them. As I've spent the last few years researching and thinking deeply about the lasting impact of the school bus and its future possibilities, this framing of privilege on school buses has sat uncomfortably with me. It should sit uncomfortably with you too. The kids being warned were Black and brown youths voluntarily getting onto buses much earlier than their peers in an attempt to get a higher-quality schooling experience. So the threats of taking away bus-riding "privileges" should be recognized as racially fraught, even if they were not intended as such.

We owe so much more to current students than the current school buses and systems of busing currently offer, even if they were operating efficiently and consistently. The school bus illuminates how the imagination of educational policy makers has failed for far too long. Particularly as the world continues to recover from a global pandemic, a steady march—or idling crawl—back to "normal" schooling operations beckons kids and drivers back on the ever-familiar bus.

What a shame. The billions wasted on ineffective online and digital educational technologies could have improved analog interactions. I say this not as a tech-fearing Luddite. Frankly, I first took on the study described in chapter 2 because I was excited about the possibilities of digitally enabling powerful and meaningful learning for kids stuck on buses each day. I believe that digital tools *can* help improve academic and social learning opportunities in schools and on buses. But they can only achieve this when they are used in support of relationships and when students are at the center of how expertise is shared and enacted. As a kind of extreme, buses literally find students in one place and physically move them at the whims and demands of adults. We have worried about ridding ourselves of the "antiquated shackles" of past practices of learning and schooling in nearly every corner of public education, *except* for the school bus. Inequalities in schools perpetuate the need for the very technologies that reinforce them. It is a circular logic that breaks down when held up to close scrutiny: we need buses because schooling systems are inequitable, and because schooling systems are inequitable, we need buses. The pandemic temporarily broke one-half of the chain of this logic, but the magnetism that binds technocratic solutions to sociopolitical ills is a strong one, and it will take more than an interest in global competitiveness to wrench us out of the complacency with busing technologies.

For nearly three years, school communities have spoken of the fear of "learning loss" during a global pandemic, as if any such thing is even remotely the primary concern when the emotional toll of the lives lost and ravaged by the pandemic is not addressed in schools right now. Setting this point aside, if our society were *actually* concerned about learning loss, we might consider the kinds of time, utility, and joy lost by students every day in the thousands of hours they spend gazing at a world passing by them from inside a school bus.

This book has been an ongoing argument that busing technology operates in two ways: as a mechanical device that drolly brings students from one place to another and as a social tool for addressing school desegregation. And although I think there are innovative ways in which these two technologies operate separately and synergistically, I also am eager for us to find these tools obsolete in a more imaginative system of schooling. As you inevitably witness the next school bus rumble past you, I invite you to wonder how else we might redefine how schooling and technology intermix and where they might take us.

Acknowledgments

This book would not be possible without the support, patience, and humor of the young people who let me learn alongside them on school buses. I am grateful for their brilliance amid the ongoing tolls aboard and because of the biggest form of educational technology to shape our schooling systems.

This work also depended on the incredible contributions and insights of my research team, including Stephanie Robillard, Miroslav Suzara, and Jorge Garcia, and assistance from Kathryn Ribay. The research in this book also could not have taken place without the support and outreach of Eric Hartwig and Michelle Nayfack.

Leah Pennywark and Eric Lundgren at University of Minnesota Press provided crucial guidance for this work. Support for the time and research shared throughout this book was provided by the Stanford-Sequoia K–12 Research Collaborative and by the Stanford Impact Lab Design Fellowship.

Friends and colleagues offered ongoing advice for this work, including Dehanza Rogers, Christopher Gutierrez, Nicole Mirra, Karli Stander, Gary Orfield, Larry Cuban, Jennifer Langer-Osuna, Ramon Martinez, and Jonathan Rosa.

My father-in-law, Greg, asked important questions about safety protocols and cleaning agents for public school buses. His dedicated concern about bus standards and health helped shape how I approached some of the work in chapter 3.

My daughters Joey and Stella were gleeful to sing the song from which this book's title and chapter titles originate. And, finally, I am grateful for Alexandria for so many reasons. Most salient to this book is her powerful reminder of the problematic representation of gender in the same song. Here's to composing better verses of "Wheels on the Bus" in the future.

(Continued from page iii)

Forerunners: Ideas First

Arne De Boever
Against Aesthetic Exceptionalism

Steve Mentz
Break Up the Anthropocene

John Protevi
Edges of the State

Matthew J. Wolf-Meyer
Theory for the World to Come: Speculative Fiction and Apocalyptic Anthropology

Nicholas Tampio
Learning versus the Common Core

Kathryn Yusoff
A Billion Black Anthropocenes or None

Kenneth J. Saltman
The Swindle of Innovative Educational Finance

Ginger Nolan
The Neocolonialism of the Global Village

Joanna Zylinska
The End of Man: A Feminist Counterapocalypse

Robert Rosenberger
Callous Objects: Designs against the Homeless

William E. Connolly
Aspirational Fascism: The Struggle for Multifaceted Democracy under Trumpism

Chuck Rybak
UW Struggle: When a State Attacks Its University

Clare Birchall
Shareveillance: The Dangers of Openly Sharing and Covertly Collecting Data

la paperson
A Third University Is Possible

Kelly Oliver
Carceral Humanitarianism: Logics of Refugee Detention

P. David Marshall
The Celebrity Persona Pandemic

Antero Garcia is associate professor in the Graduate School of Education at Stanford University. He is the author of *Good Reception: Teens, Teachers, and Mobile Media in a Los Angeles High School*, and *Critical Foundations in Young Adult Literature: Challenging Genres* and coauthor of books including *Annotation* and *Tuned-In Teaching: Centering Youth Culture for an Active and Just Classroom*.